NEW AGE LIES TO WOMEN

NEW AGE LIES TO WOMEN

WANDA MARRS

LTP Living Truth Publishers
8103 Shiloh Court • Austin, Texas 78745

Scripture quotations are from the King James Version of The
Holy Bible.

Cover design: Wanda Marrs

Second printing, 1990

Printed in the United States of America

Library of Congress Catalog Card Number 89-063724

ISBN 0-9620086-3-X

ACKNOWLEDGEMENTS

So many wonderful people have helped me with this important book. How can I ever repay my husband, Texe, for his wisdom, insight, and advice! He carefully labored with me, researching and helping me organize and present *New Age Lies to Women* in a manner that befits a subject of such profound implications.

I am grateful, too, for the efforts of Ken Greene, our dedicated business manager, who did so much in the production of the book. Also, thanks go to Mike Motal, whose computer skills were a God-send.

TABLE OF

Contents

Acknowledgements   v

Preface   ix

1   Satan's Mistress and Her New Age Lies   13
        to Women

2   From Hollywood to Capitol Hill: Satan's   33
        Magnificent All-Star Cast

3   The Great Sex Carnival: Lust and Abandon   51
        in the New Age

4   The Unholy Trinity: Father of Light, Bride of   75
        Darkness and Son of Perdition

5   Unmasking the Hidden Darkness   87

6   Sins of Mystery Babylon   101

7   The Goddess is Back! She Lives!   123

8   And Her Son Shall Have the Number 666   137

9   The Goddess and the Serpent   151

10 The One Most Terrible Secret   165

11 Initiation: The Seduction of Women   181

12 You, Too, Can Become a Goddess   193

13 The Lifestyle of the Liberated Aquarian Woman   205

14 Back to the Future   221

15 The Beautiful Woman: Crystal Clear Answers   235
        to Dark New Age Lies

Footnotes   242

About the Author

For More Information

Preface

What is the *One* most terrible secret that the New Age leadership definitely does not want you to know? That's the focus of this in-depth, revealing book. Something very alarming, incredibly important, and quite horrible is loose in today's world. The beast from the catacombs is slouching his way toward Jerusalem, and every woman lies directly across his path. You, too, are his target, his chosen victim, and believe me, he has you in his sight.

For over four years I have investigated the New Age movement and religion. During this time, I have had many occasions to observe its insidious and sinister nature first-hand. Clearly, the seduction of women is top priority on Satan's hidden New Age agenda. But men, too, are certainly not excluded. It's just that Satan well knows that the feminine hands that rock the cradle have tremendous influence. He knows that once he conquers a woman and brings her heart and soul into captivity, he can then move quickly to grasp her husband, plunder her children, and gather into his dark kingdom her entire family and circle of friends.

The enslavement of one woman by the Adversary creates a chain reaction of deception, followed by widespread misery and despair.

For this reason, unmasking the *New Age Lies to Women* is an undertaking of paramount significance. Satan does not attack women haphazardly and with half-hearted measures. He has set forth a meticulous, well laid out battle plan and deliberately analyzed each of our weaknesses. He knows of our vulnerabilities and our festering open wounds, and often he has keen insight into our innermost desires and cravings. All this he uses against us . . . to great advantage.

Satan's New Age Plan is intricately connected with Bible prophecy. We cannot uncover his dark plot and expose his passion for our destruction unless we examine Satan's efforts in light of scripture. The Evil One has no power on his own, except what God temporarily grants to him. His fate is sealed and his destiny can be understood only by going to the Word and seeing what God has prophesied will occur in these last days.

However, once we do turn our attention to God's marvelous prophetic Word, all the pieces of the puzzle quickly fall into place. Every lie of Satan suddenly unravels, and the stark horror of what is planned for you, I, and every woman comes transparently--and miraculously--into view.

New Age Lies to Women is, therefore, a book of secrets. But if you are one of His children, these are secrets that our Lord and Savior, Jesus Christ, wants you to know. He himself told His disciples: "For there is nothing covered that shall not be revealed, neither hid that shall not be known" (Luke 8:17).

You do not have to become a hellish statistic, a battered casualty of Satan's New Age spiritual warfare. You can know about his wicked designs and aims for your life. And you can know of his grotesque objectives for your loved ones and even for our nation and the planet. This is why God gave us His prophetic Word, so we would not be taken by surprise.

Startling Facts and Mysteries Revealed

In the 256 pages of this book you will discover facts so startling that were it not for the security we have in Christ Jesus, your heart could well be overcome with fear and dread. Here are just a few of the mysteries you will find revealed and the prophetic riddles that will be solved in *New Age Lies to Women:*

● The concealed truth about the Mystery Woman of Sin whom Satan has chosen as his mistress and queen.

● The profoundly wicked scheme of Satan's New Age to initiate you and every woman on earth into his service and kingdom, so that you can become his betrothed, his "bride of darkness."

● The actual names and identities of the leaders--the "movers and shakers" of the New Age--the rich, famous, influential . . . and *sinister* men and women who are at the very forefront in promoting a New Age World Religion and a One World Order.

● The astonishing New Age revival of the Mystery Babylon religion and the return of the sensual Goddess who today presides over the New Age movement.

● The revelation of an *unholy trinity* composed of Father of Light (Lucifer), Mother (the "awakened" Goddess of Mystery Babylon), and their perverse and deadly Son of Perdition (the Antichrist).

Also revealed in *New Age Lies to Women:* The identity of the beast that rises out of the sea (Revelation 13:1); why the New Age promotes bisexuality and gay rights; the

New Age "Dream Sex" audiotapes which encourage ungodly intimate relations with demon spirits; the restoration of holy sex rituals and ceremonies of ancient Babylon, Rome, and Greece by "Temple" priestesses at New Age worship centers throughout the U.S.A.; the Catholic priests who envision "God" as a sexy, playful "voluptuous and delicious" temptress; the bestselling book--often called a "Christian Classic"--that was literally written by demon spirits; why Alcoholics Anonymous, other 12-step programs, modern psychology, and the co-dependency myth are all dangerous to your spiritual health and pathways to demonic possession; and the New Age Plan to soon have every man on earth kneel and submit to Woman.

The New Age delusion is strong. As one relieved woman who had escaped the magnetic attraction of the New Age and found Jesus explained:

"Sometimes I'm completely baffled, embarrassed and amazed that I could have gone that far and fell into such a destructive spell. But it's such a gradual and insidious type of hypnosis and so subtle, that an individual is not aware it's happening. You have to experience it to understand."

Everything said above is true except the very last sentence. The New Age is *not* something "you have to experience to understand." Armed with the knowledge and information found in this book, and through the saving power of our Lord Jesus Christ, the holy Lamb of God, you *can* recognize Satan's lies, and expose his evil tactics . . . You *can* choose life.

Wanda Marrs
Austin, Texas

ONE

Satan's Mistress and Her New Age Lies to Women

So he carried me away in the spirit into the wilderness: and I saw a woman sit upon a Scarlet coloured beast, full of names of blasphemy. . . . And the woman was arrayed in purple and scarlet colour, and decked with gold and precious stones and pearls, having a golden cup in her hand full of abominations and filthiness of her fornication.

(Revelation 17:3-4)

I was . . . perhaps the daughter of a thousand shining stars . . . the shakti, the potent female energy that can change the earth . . . the portal to the past and the future, a sanctuary for incarnating souls, a pleasure field of heaven, a sweet and beautiful flower, complete with perfume and nectar, surely worthy of being worshipped and kissed.

Rickie Moore
A Goddess in My Shoes

You've come a long way baby," so the ad goes. Yes, women have come a long way since Eve took a bite of the forbidden fruit in the Garden of Eden. But regrettably, for the vast majority of women today, the spiritual journey has brought them back full circle. Just as the New Age pictures the eternal serpent biting its tail, modern woman has returned to the beginning.

The New Age, however, revels and delights in the accomplishment of "Mother Eve." Her act was a divine step making it possible for all women to become goddesses. Her inheritance is a positive treasure for us today, it is claimed. Hail Eve!

In the garden, Satan, under the guise of the serpent, captivated Eve and charmed her, literally, to death. His was the Great Lie. As women today catapult bravely toward the twenty-first century, Satan continues to work his magical charms and tell his smooth, convincing lies. He is now aided by millions of human helpers. His New Age religionists range across the face of America and the globe. Once again, the Great Lie is being whispered to women.

In the Garden, Adam and Eve disobeyed the loving God who had created them and had given them prosperity and every good and perfect thing for their enjoyment and contentment. The Great Lie of the New Age also tragically results in disobedience to God. Ultimately, each woman who buys into Satan's deceptive Lie is sucked into a life of sinfulness and evil. Her greatest loss, however, comes from the fact that she is separated from the only true source of eternal happiness--the Lord Jesus Christ, King of Kings and Lord of Lords.

The Hunger of Eve

It is little wonder that the New Age credits Eve as being the founding Mother of their religion. It was Eve, these false teachers say, who began woman's (and man's) journey to self-divinity and godhood. Eve, therefore, is held up as a goddess figure by many New Age leaders. It is in the image of Eve that all women are to be molded and conformed.

Since Eve in the garden gave in to her carnal, lustful, and fleshly desires, then, the New Age reasons, you and I, women of the late twentieth century, also should give in to these same sensual desires. The reward for Eve was *sensual knowledge*, a reward greatly valued in New Age theology. The New Age is the ultimate sensual religion. Its believers are in reality members of a *cult*--a cult based on the fleshly experiences of sexuality and sensuousness. Every woman who is a member of the New Age Cult aspires to become like Eve.

Barbara Marx Hubbard, prominent New Age world leader and former democratic party candidate for vice president of the U.S.A., has even written a book entitled *The Hunger of Eve*. All New Age women, writes Hubbard, are consumed by the hunger of Eve to pluck and eat the forbidden fruit off the tree in the garden:

> I have always identified with Eve. . . . Throughout all of human history, we have been reaching for this mystical tree. Now we collectively stand at this fateful tree, driven here by our hunger. . . . Together we can create new worlds of undreamt possibilities for all people. We stand at that point in history where the hunger can be fulfilled . . .[1]

The New Age wants you and I to believe that by surrendering to the overwhelming hunger within, by submitting our bodies and minds to the insatiable lust and wanton desire that so often war in our flesh for control, we can reach the spiritual mountain top. Through ecstasy and letting go, we can transform our lives and achieve peaks of unbridled passion which vault us into new heights of cosmic consciousness. In effect, you and I can become a *goddess*!

The Perfect New Age Role Model for Women

Women who either unwittingly or on purpose are lured into the New Age follow after an alluring and desirable role model. Subtly and craftily, they are programmed into the image of New Age woman. And that image is based on that of the Goddess of Mystery Babylon, more accurately described as the Mother Goddess.

To New Age woman, the Goddess brilliantly reigns over all. Yet, behind her outward appearance of magnetic allure lies a dark hidden secret.

To the initiated New Age woman, the Goddess is life itself. She is the spirit that permeates the universe. Her image is one of sexual power, ecstasy, and spiritual mastery. She is deity. The work of transforming oneself into the Goddess is therefore a work of holiness. Every New Age woman moves, walks and talks, and has her very being in the Goddess.

Just who is this Goddess who is the role model, the quintessential spiritual entity, toward whose heights of perfection every woman should aspire? She is, answers the New Age, the very same Mystery Woman who, after Eve, was glorified as the Mother Goddess in ancient Babylon.

The Woman Astride the Beast

To discover the true identity of the Mother Goddess, to unravel her mysterious nature and understand her great lie, it is necessary that we turn to the pages of our Holy Bible. There, in Revelation 17:3-6, we come face-to-face with the New Age Goddess. Her name is *Mystery Babylon*:

> So he carried me away in the spirit into the wilderness: and I saw a woman sit upon a scarlet coloured beast, full of names of blasphemy, having seven heads and ten horns.

> And the woman was arrayed in purple and scarlet colour, and decked with gold and precious stones and pearls, having a golden cup in her hand full of abominations and filthiness of her fornication:

> And upon her forehead was a name written, MYSTERY, BABYLON THE GREAT, THE MOTHER OF HARLOTS AND ABOMINATIONS OF THE EARTH.

> And I saw the woman drunken with the blood of the saints, and with the blood of the martyrs of Jesus: and when I saw her, I wondered with great admiration.

Could this be true? Is this bloody Woman of Sin here, now? Is her ungodly and grotesque, murderous religion today called the "New Age?" Is Bible Prophecy being fulfilled in an amazing way as Satan's last days world religion rapidly fills the Earth with its sorcery and occultism?

Though the New Age Religion comes to us in a glittery and glamorous package, promising women the keys to intellectual mysteries and the revealing of the secrets of the eternal, could it be that beneath all of the shiny and trendy practices--all the colorful tinsel--that the New Age is nothing more nor less than Mystery, Babylon the Great, the Mother of Harlots and Abominations of the Earth? Is *she* the Mother Goddess of the New Age? And what part does Satan play in all this? If the New Age is presided over by a goddess, then is she not *wed* to a god? And is it not true that her lord and master is the lord of this world-- that is, Lucifer?

The Shocking Truth is Revealed

You will discover in the pages of this book the answers to all of these probing questions. As the shocking truth is exposed to light, this astonishing fact stands out: The New Age movement and religion *is* Mystery Babylon, the last days world-wide church of Satan. Moreover, this church is presided over by a Queen, the Mystery Woman of Sin. She is aptly described as Satan's Mistress, and she is an ambitious and lust-filled, voluptuous and beautiful goddess.

Satan has dressed his mistress in a spectacular gown of purple and scarlet color. He has decked her with precious stones and pearls and placed in her hand a golden cup filled with abominations and filthiness of her fornication.

She is the mother of harlots and he is her consort and live-in companion.

Now, let me unveil to you yet another, even more profound dark mystery. The greatest secret of all is that *Satan wants you and I and every woman to be just like her.* He wants you and I to become his mistress, his unholy bride. Through a process of New Age initiation into the Mysteries which now have been restored by the New Age, Satan seeks to become your bridegroom. First, however, it is necessary that you prepare yourself as his betrothed. If you are to become his bride and lover, you must have a complete makeover. You must wrap yourself in all of the blackened glory and all of the wicked, infamous majesty befitting of Satan's Woman. *You must become the Goddess.*

Yes, the Goddess is back. If you do not belong to Christ Jesus, she is you! You may choose to frantically deny this horrible fact. You may cry out in anger and frustration that you do not *choose* to be Satan's Mistress. But all this will be of no avail. Jesus said you and I cannot serve two masters. Who, then, is your Lord? Who is *your* bridegroom?

Mystery Babylon is Restored

The restoration of Mystery Babylon in a new setting as today's New Age World Religion has been achieved with shocking suddenness. Through Bible prophecy God revealed to His elect that the last days movement of Satan would be a revival of Mystery Babylon. Satan has no power of His own. None other than what God has prophesied. Therefore, he has no option but to awaken, hone, sharpen, and polish up all of the filthy and perverse teachings, practices, and religious doctrines of ancient

THE RETURN OF THE CHRIST
AS A WOMAN HAS OCCURRED

Rejoice! The CHRIST, our sacred friend; who is also expected as Krishana, Maitreya Budda, and other names, has reappeared in Boston as:

MATA MAITREYA
THE MOTHER OF THE WORLD

Come and join us in aiding the CHRIST to bring peace and enlightenment to Mother Earth.

THE MAITREYA WORLD FOUNDATION, INC.
63 COOLIDGE ROAD
BOSTON, MASS. 02134

At Saint John the Divine Cathedral in New York City, the largest cathedral in America, the Episcopal Priest James P. Morton took the figure of Jesus off the crucifix and put up a female named "Christa." Meanwhile, in Boston, a group claiming that "Christ" has returned--and she's a woman--placed this ad in various national magazines.

Babylon, and resurrect them for today. Naturally, he seeks to give them a fresh coat of paint, a new image. This is why he calls his last days world religion and movement the *New* Age. But of course, it is not the New Age, but an old age religion, one that was described with great precision and accuracy in Bible prophecy.

What evidence do I have that the Mother Goddess has been awakened and that Mystery Babylon is here, now?

The undeniable fact that Mystery Babylon has come to life and that the wound of the beast has been healed (Revelation 13:3) confronts us almost everywhere we turn. The full dimensions of Satan's success in raising from its deep sleep the serpentine religion of the Whore of Babylon shock our senses. When we survey the amazing spectacles that are taking place today across the American landscape, our faith in God's word becomes revitalized and sure. Just as God's prophets wrote, Mystery Babylon has again risen its ugly head.

The Goddess returns with the Great Lie of the Adversary, that we shall be as gods. She also brings with her in her modern incarnation a multitude of lesser lies. We will unmask many of those lies in this book, as we tear off the veil of the mystery woman and expose her glamour, sensuality and outer beauty for what it is: a deceptive mask. Tear off the mask, unveil the goddess and her truly hideous nature is revealed: She is a creature from the pit. Exposed, she reverts to her true nature: A swirling and tumultuous mass of lithe, twisting and turning asps and serpents.

The Harlot is Back--The Amazing Evidence

Let us then examine some of the mountainous evidence that unmasks the staggering reality of the New Age as the revival of the Goddess, the return of Satan's Mystery

Babylon religion. I believe you will be both revolted and amazed as you read the true stories that follow. As you do, ask yourself: Is not the harlot of Mystery Babylon alive and well today? Does she not reign over modern woman? And what of Jesus' warning, "When these things begin to come to pass, then look up, and lift up your heads, for your redemption draweth nigh" (Luke 21:28). Are these not the signs of the soon coming and return of Christ Jesus? Has the devil indeed "come down upon us, having great wrath, because he knoweth that he hath but a short time" (Revelation 13:12)? Finally, if the momentous events that are revealed in these pages are occurring with such frequency and regularity today, is it not time that each of us recognize that the end is, indeed, very, very near? Knowing this, what should be our attitude and how should we conduct our lives--as women, as mothers, and as children of the living God?

Satanic Ecstasy . . . The New Age Frequency

The arousal of illicit sexual desires in women is one of Satan's most powerful weapons. In Babylon, his religion was built on a foundation of sexual ecstasy. Holy, ritual sex was engaged in by men and women as a means to becoming one with the Goddess. Through sexual intercourse, they hoped to achieve a higher state of divine consciousness.

Is this practice being restored today in the New Age? Read below the incredible, yet commonplace, true account of one woman's modern-day return to the religious depravity of Mystery Babylon.

> I knew spiritual did not exclude sexual. The tantric and Taoist approaches to spiritual sexuality appealed to me.

When I heard they emphasized the need for a man to keep the woman absolutely satisfied, I said sign me up! I wanted to become an enlistee.

We started off slowly, going to every available workshop, buying all the books written about it, and setting aside time . . .

Our first tantra course paid off. Now . . . I can have a "jade garden" or a "lovely lotus," if I choose. His (male body part--word deleted) became a magic scepter, a healing wand, or . . . a jewel. Just singing, "The jewel is in the lotus" was a turn on.

Through successive heights of ecstasy, we began to see visions with our minds, fill them with our hearts and dream them simultaneously. Yoga had prepared us individually for what we were experiencing together.

I was . . . perhaps the daughter of a thousand shining stars . . . the *Shakti*, the potent female energy that can change the face of the earth . . . the portal to the past and the future, a sanctuary for incarnating souls, a pleasure field of heaven, a sweet and beautiful flower, complete with perfume and nectar, surely worthy of being worshiped and kissed.

I thanked the stars then for all little girls, witches, and crazy ladies . . . and for all little boys, wizards, and holy men. I didn't need anyone to tell me I was a goddess . . . I knew it!

We began our ceremony at home . . . the altar was adorned with happy yellow face flowers, and bright burning candles that illuminated pictures of our loved ones. A single, long-stemmed rose, my symbol for protection, reminded us that we could experience the mystical union with the universe . . .

We stood naked in front of the altar . . . then we took a
comfortable tantra seat and gazed long and deep into each
others eyes . . .

Then, he was on his knees in front of me . . . I stood there
looking holy and goddess-like in my new exotic belt.[2]

Horned God Come!

The following is a true account of a witchcraft ritual in
which the participants call on both Satan and his Mistress,
the Goddess, to manifest themselves. The High Priestess
of this particular witches coven, Miriam Starhawk, is no
stranger to Christianity. As unbelievable as it may seem,
she has been a guest speaker for a number of "Christian"
groups. On one occasion, she spoke to a large assemblage
of priests and nuns at a Catholic seminary. Her talk on
the "Earth Religion" was well received and applauded.[3]

It is December 21, the Winter Solstice. Starhawk and her
coven are meeting to celebrate the birthday of the sun.
There is a fire in the fireplace of the large, high-ceilinged
room. Two long snakeskins, recently shed by Starhawk's
two pet boa constrictors, are draped from the chandelier.
The twenty celebrants stand in a circle. All are nude. The
women outnumber the men.

Starhawk turns to the outside of the circle, faces east,
raises a wooden-handled knife and begins to summon the
spirits:

Hail, Guardians of the Watchtowers of the East,
Powers of air--
We invoke you and call you,

Great golden eagle of the dawn
Star-seeker!
Whirlwind!
Rising sun!
Come to us!
By the air that is Her breath
Send forth your spirit
Be here now!

She then traces a five-pointed star in the air.

She walks around the circle, pausing at the south, the west, and the north to invoke the powers of all points of the compass. When she returns to where she began, she announces that the circle is cast.

The women and men now sit cross-legged on the floor and Starhawk begins her invocation to the Goddess:

Queen of the night
Queen of the moon
Queen of the stars
Queen of the horns
Queen of the earth
Bring to us the child of light.

Night sky rider
Silver shining one
Lady of wild things
Silver wheel
North star
Circle
Crescent
Moon-bright
Singer
Changer!
Touch us!

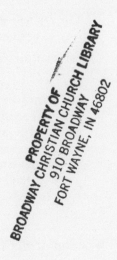

> See with our eyes
> Hear with our ears,
> Breathe with our nostrils,
> Kiss with our lips,
> Touch with our hands,
> Be here now!

The chant is a long one. Some of the other women take turns reciting their own poems--their own invocations to the Goddess.

"She is with us," Starhawk announces.

One of the men beats a drum to invoke the Horned God. This chant is much less elaborate.

> Seed sower grain reborn
> Horned God Come!
> Seed sower grain reborn
> Horned God Come!

The drumming is a simple, but powerful three-beat thump.

"He is here," declares Starhawk, and the drumming stops.

She turns to a man on her left and kisses him lightly on the lips. "Thou art God," she says. "Thou art Goddess," he replies. He turns and passes the kiss to the woman next to him. "Thou art Goddess," he tells her. The kiss is passed around the circle amid smiles and some giggles. The first phase of their ritual is complete.[4]

Worship of the Idol of the Goddess of Destruction

The Bible warns us not to anger and defy God by the unholy worship of idols. Today, idol worship is back, as this account of a ceremony aboard a ship owned and operated by Scientology, a New Age religion, shockingly demonstrates.

The ceremonies were done below deck in a section of the ship that had been used as a classroom for crew study.

There a large idol of (Mother Goddess) Kali had been erected. It looked very solid and real and was painted in gold.

The only light in this huge otherwise empty training room, down in the bowels of the ship, was the flickering of a few candles.

Sandra Wilson was one of those who went through the ceremony. She was brought forward and led up to Kali.

In front of Kali had been erected a cardboard representation of an organization, a shoe box with painted-on windows and so on. Some of the crew filed in ceremoniously, dressed in monks' cloaks and carrying burning torches which left a strong smell permeating the room.

Sandra was handed a hammer and commanded: "Your proposed plan for your organization would have destroyed it. You are a student of Kali, the Goddess of Destruction."

Destroy this organization!

She solemnly smashed the mocked-up organization with the hammer. Since the crime of destruction of a Scientology organization is indoctrinated heavily into Scientologists as the most evil act imaginable, to do so-- even in effigy--was an excruciatingly painful experience.

Then, following the orders relayed from L. Ron Hubbard (Scientology's leader), she bowed down and chanted to the idol, admitting her "evil intention" to destroy her local organization, and dipped her hands in blood (or a solution which was a very good imitation), and smeared it onto the idol, after which chicken bones were strung around her neck.

She came out of there in shock and was overcome with grief for some 48 hours.

As I watched her in this terrible state I was quietly outraged by what had happened. But I hid my outrage; even doubted its validity.

I had been thoroughly trained that if I were being critical of L. Ron Hubbard or his actions, it must be because of my own hidden misdeeds and crimes.[5]

The Baptism of a Satanic Witch

In the ceremonies of pagan religions, baptisms-- counterfeits of the Christian sacrament--were conducted as rites of initiation. Below is the modern-day account of one such dark baptism, exactly as it is recorded in the book, *The Satanic Witch*, by Anton LaVey, head of the Church of Satan. LaVey has declared that the goal of his unholy church is to usher in a "New Age." (The person being baptized is LaVey's daughter, Zeena, and the words are hers.)

My baptism was indeed the reversal of a Christian baptism. Instead of being dunked into a cold bath by a strange, sexless man to be cleansed of "original sin," we celebrated man and nature as they really are.

As I sat wearing the red robe my mother made that morning, I toyed with the Baphomet amulet dangling around my neck (this image of the Satanic goat was hand-crafted for me by the pioneering survivalist Kurt Saxon, a founding member of the Church of Satan). Imperiously, I surveyed the sea of black-hooded celebrants. It took me a few years to realize that some of them may have been more fascinated with the naked woman sprawled on the altar than with me. The gothic strains of a Hammond organ echoed against the black and red walls. Calmly chewing on a stick of Trident fruit-flavored gum, I delighted in being the focal point of all this activity.

My father, the High Priest, raised his ceremonial sword in benediction. I felt a great sense of warmth and respect. How many people can honestly say they have this feeling at any point in their life? "I have something they don't," I thought proudly, in keeping with the indulgent philosophy of Satanism. Since that night I understood what it means to be a Satanic Witch, a woman who makes full use of her feminine wiles. Throughout my life I would replay the words intoned during my baptism:

The many footed walkers give you the strength, the power of red fang and claw, all the madly dancing demons fill you with the lost knowledge of ancient ones. Small sorceress, the most natural and true magician, your tiny hands have the power to pull the living heavens down and from its shards build a monument to your own sweet indulgence. . . . And with these others in the devil's fane, you will so cause the heads of men to reel and spin, you will fill them with desire. And so we dedicate your life to love, to passion, to indulgence, and to Satan and the way of darkness, fane. Hail Zeena! Hail Satan![6]

This is the Baphomet, the horned goat god whose amulet Zeena wore around her neck during a satanic baptism. Note the bisexual nature, the word "shive" (or the Hindu god Shiva) on the right arm, and the mixture of good and evil represented by the light and dark crescent moons.

The Asclepian Healing Temple Experience

Asclepios, the Greek god of healing, was said to be the son of Apollo, the Greek sun god. Is the worship of these ancient deities a distant relic of the bizarre past? Or, could it be possible that the Mystery Babylon religion, of

SATAN'S MISTRESS   □   31

which Apollo and Asclepios were a part, is reawakening in our day? The article below, reprinted exactly as it appeared in a recent issue of the *Seattle New Times* newspaper, provides us the startling answers.

On Sunday, October 23rd, from 1-7 p.m., The Northwest Center for Holistic Medicine will be magically transformed into an ancient Greek Temple dedicated to the God of Healing, Asclepios.

Imagine entering a temple, purifying yourself in the sacred showers, hot tub and sauna, and being anointed and massaged with exotic oils. You will receive sacred guidance, laying on of hands and crystal healing from the temple priest and priestesses. Astrology, tarot and past-life readings will illuminate your soul's path.

You will perform rituals and make offerings to the gods and be released from your sufferings by creating a vision of your own wholeness. Ambrosial nectar and manna from heaven will delight your palate as well. You haven't experienced any thing like this for lifetimes!

Inspired by the Asclepian vision presented in Jean Houston's recent book, *In Search of the Beloved*, the staff of the Northwest Center for Holistic Medicine will draw upon their priestly healing and oracular skills to intercede for you with the gods and provide you with an experience specifically designed to heal you in body, mind and spirit. By going beyond your normal context and creating a space and time totally devoted to healing on all levels, you will have the opportunity to understand yourself and experience your wholeness in a new way.

All are welcome in the Temple. You may arrive for the Experience at one of three times, 1, 3, or 5 p.m. Reservations are encouraged as space is limited. A

donation to Asclepios of $15 ensures you admission and
grants you access to all of the wonders of the Temple. Plan
to spend two hours or more enjoying all the heavenly
delights which have been prepared for you. Please wear
comfortable white or pastel-colored clothing, robes or a
toga as you prefer, and bring a swimsuit, sandals and towel.
You may bring an offering of flowers, fruit or a sacred
object for the altar of Asclepios if you wish. Please call for
reservations or more information.[7]

The Evidence is Staggering . . . She's Returned!

The evidence demands our attention: *sacred ritual sex,
witchcraft invocations, unholy Satanic baptisms, idol
worship*--America and the entire world are on a collision
course with Bible prophecy. The New Age has once again
lit the fires of ancient paganism and revitalized the
mystical Goddess Religion.

In Chapter Fourteen, "Back to the Future," I'll present further startling evidence that the New Age is simply
returning us to Babylon. We'll examine the incredible
demonstrations in today's New Age of counterfeit speaking in tongues, carnal relations with demonic spirits,
visions of the Goddess, and more.

But for now, let us turn our focus to those who are
promoting this unholy reawakening of the Mystery Woman of Babylon. Who are the men and women, New Age
leaders and enthusiasts, who seek to rebuild the Tower of
Babel? As we shall see, they are legion and they are
powerful and influential. From Hollywood to Capitol Hill,
they roam the modern landscape, offering us what one
person has called "a return to the future--the Dawn of a
New Age."

From Hollywood To Capitol Hill: Satan's Magnificent All-Star Cast

Ye are of your father the devil, and the lusts of your father ye will do: he was a murderer from the beginning and abode not in the truth, because there is no truth in him. When he speaketh a lie, he speaketh of his own: for he is a liar and the father of it.

Jesus (John 8:44)

The Christ (Lord Maitreya) needs disciples and men of goodwill who can help push humanity successfully and more quickly into New Age consciousness. Yes, our civilization is dying. Let us move on into the new day and begin now to build that new civilization which the Aquarian Age will surely bring. Let us dare to be spiritual pioneers. The torch of light and truth has been passed to us as well as to the youth of the present generation.

Foster Bailey
Running God's Plan

Everyone is going New Age!" This was what one enthusiastic supporter of the New Age recently told a TV reporter. To prove her point, she began to rattle off names of the rich and famous, the jet-setters and glamor crowd who are involved in the New Age movement: She mentioned movie stars Don Johnson, Melanie Griffith, Robert Redford, Sigourney Weaver, Shirley MacLaine, Patrick Duffy, and Allie Sheedy. TV stars named included Phylicia Rashad, Valerie Harper, Linda Evans, Lisa Bonet, and Sharon Gless. Singers named: Willie Nelson, Tina Turner, Michael Jackson, Cher, and John Denver. Oh yes, the name of Prince Phillip came up, along with Her Highness Juliana, of the Netherlands.

The list was impressive and no doubt left the viewing audience gaping in wide-eyed amazement. It does indeed seem that the whole world is going New Age. The list of avid and dedicated New Age disciples and supporters is growing at an unbelievable pace. Moreover, the list is not composed only of Hollywood and entertainment types. Political superstars and world leaders have eagerly joined the ranks of the New Age army. So, too, have world renowned scientists, authors, psychologists, astronauts, educators, Wall Street investors, and industrialists.

Today, there is no area of a woman's life in which she can escape the intrusion of New Ageism. If she turns on her TV she finds sitcoms and dramas alike saturated with New Age themes. Movies are worse. Her kids' lives, too, are permeated with New Age occultism in school curricula, cartoons, toys, rock music--even comic books and library books. A multitude of women's books, especially fantasy novels and fiction but also so-called "Christian" devotional books come laced with subtle and not so subtle New Age story-lines. Even a trip to the doctor's office may well result in an uninvited lesson on New Age, holistic medicine.

Working wives are being forced to attend New Age thinking seminars and training courses by employers. Meanwhile, their husbands are having their minds filled with such New Age ideas as "attracting prosperity consciousness" and how to become a tennis whiz or master a golf swing through the use of New Age visualization and meditation.

Moreover, women are told that "all" the human relations "experts" and all the glittery in-crowd are "into" the New Age and that they are missing out on the excitement and mystery if they, too, don't get involved in crystals, spirit channeling, higher consciousness, tantric sex, yoga, tarot cards, and so forth.

Millions of women are being sucked in by the massive waves of publicity generated by the New Age celebrity elite. If you doubt that women can be influenced by celebrity endorsements, just consider the widespread popularity and massive circulation of such supermarket spell-binders and gossip sheets as *National Enquirer, The National Examiner, Star, Weekly World News,* and *People* magazine. Then check out the ratings of such TV extravaganzas as *Lifestyles of the Rich and Famous, 20/20, Entertainment Tonight, The Phil Donahue Show, Oprah Winfrey* and so on, which so often focus on the personal lives and interests of the rich and famous.

Psychiatrists like M. Scott Peck and psychologists such as Lee Buscaglia add to the mania for New Ageism on the part of women. Meanwhile, New Age books by medical doctors such as Bernie Siegel rocket to the top of the *New York Time's* bestseller lists, further drawing women into the allure of New Age occultism. Satan is having a field day!

New Age Workers of Darkness

If he is to capture the souls of women, and do so by his target date of 2000 A.D., Satan knows that he needs a huge army of expertly trained and highly motivated workers of darkness. The Bible tells us that Satan seeks to deceive the whole world and that he works his devilish plan and purposes through human agents whom he subverts and captures (Revelation 12:9; II Timothy 2:26; Ephesians 2:2; II Thessalonians 2).

On August 16-17, 1987, during the world-wide Harmonic Convergence event, the New Age leadership launched a major offensive designed to usher in the New Age Kingdom through the efforts of Satan's fast growing horde of human agents. A five-year mobilization plan, it is called the *Campaign for the Earth*. Its leader is Jose Arguelles, a man who has established an international network of New Age organizations, groups, and churches.[1]

According to Arguelles, the Campaign for the Earth was made possible primarily because of the fabulous success and spiraling growth of the New Age since 1970, the year the first major New Age global event, Earth Day, exceeded all expectations. The new five-year plan of the New Age (note the fascinating parallel with Communist Russia's Five Year Plans), says Arguelles, began in 1987 with a "new world order infrastructure." By 1989, with the help of the world's media, the Campaign for the Earth was said to be in full swing. And by 1992, Arguelles boasts, "it will be evident that a new era has dawned."[2]

Judging by the sensational growth in New Age support over the past decades and especially since 1987, the New Age Plan to seduce and destroy women has apparently shifted into high gear and is now in its final momentous stages. Even a decade ago, the networking of New Agers had grown so monstrously enlarged that New Age leader Marilyn Ferguson bragged that the "Aquarian Conspirators" (her term) are now everywhere:

> There are legions of conspirators. They are in corporations, universities, and hospitals, on the faculties of public schools, in factories and doctor's offices, in state and federal agencies, on city councils and the White House staff, in state legislatures, in volunteer organizations, in virtually all arenas of policy-making in the country.[3]

Since Ferguson wrote this, hundreds of thousands of New Age conspirators have come out of the closet. Now it's trendy and fashionable to reject Jesus and "Christian fundamentalism" while embracing New Age teachings and beliefs.

More Than Half a Billion New Age Supporters

How many men and women today are active supporters of the New Age? Just four years ago, John Randolph Price, head of the powerful Planetary Commission, asserted:

> We now estimate that more than half-a-billion (New Age) believers are on the planet at this time working in various religious groups--and that New Thought concepts are spreading more rapidly than any other spiritual teaching . . .[4]

While the figure of 500 million--that's half-a-billion!--is itself stupendous, in recent years the ranks of the New Age workers of darkness have continued to swell and expand to reach unheralded, mind-boggling levels. On December 31, 1987, the same John Randolph Price who earlier had boasted of almost 500 million New Age believers worldwide was able to report that this number had mushroomed to a colossal 875 million! This was the astonishing number of men, women, and children who took part in a single event, the Global Mind-Link, also called World Healing Day and the Instant of Cooperation.[5]

Pleased with the tremendous global response to his call for a Global Mind-Link, Price published and sent out a bulletin "To the people and organizations in the 82 countries/principalities/ dependencies who shared their Light, Love, and Spiritual Consciousness for healing and harmonizing of Planet Earth. . . ." In the bulletin, he proclaimed an eventual victory of the New Age over the opposing forces of fundamentalism:

> You are the Master Builders of the New Civilization, and our work shall not be in vain. . . . A New World will be revealed.[6]

Even if Price's numbers--875 million or more--are suspect and over-inflated, certainly there are tens and tens of millions now involved in this monstrous religion. The remarkable total numbers of New Age believers alone should be enough to jostle Christians who love Jesus and have a burden for the lost to shake off their complacency and get busy preaching the Gospel. Obviously, we are doing far too little to witness and evangelize these millions of New Age victims, many of whom have never had the opportunity to learn about Jesus our Lord.

However, the most frightening fact about the New Age is its composition. Its ranks include many of the most powerful and influential men and women in America, and the world. These determined advocates are filling up every nook, cranny, and crevice of women's lives with their evil New Age teachings, concepts, and images. Women and mothers are under the gravest assault since the days of the Old Testament era, when the pagans--spiritual ancestors of today's New Age movement--sacrificed children and adults to the consuming fires of Moloch, Baal and the other false gods invented by Satan's demons.

Wherever we turn today we discover the sinister influence of the New Age assault on women.

The Power Elite of the New Age World Religion

There is no longer any doubt that Satan has inspired his earth-bound, flesh and blood servants to go all out to entrap and snare women. Sadly, almost the whole of society has become a boiling cauldron in which ungodly New Age ingredients coagulate and bubble, releasing poisonous and deadly vapors that are choking women and robbing them of the Truth that can only be found in Christ Jesus.

Who is behind this determined but demented Satanic campaign to grab the souls of women? How did these unquestionably evil men and women succeed in ever gaining such tremendous positions of influence in society which allow them almost unbridled access to women's lives? More importantly, what are the future plans of these cunning New Age leaders? What is next to come on their unseemly, unholy agenda?

Among the most influential and powerful of the New Age elite are the individuals listed below. Note that these are men and women of great magnetism, charisma and authority; most are highly regarded and respected in the political, professional, business and religious communities. Some of the well-known names that appear below are so familiar and recognizable that their inclusion here as New Age teachers, supporters, and believers will shock and startle you. I know. I, too, have been amazed over and over at the ability of Satan's New Age lies to attract so many men and women to his cause.

Ted Turner. "We've got to get a New Age President elected!" Ted Turner told a group of "futurists" at John Denver's Windstar Community, in Colorado in 1986, referring to the upcoming United States presidential campaign.[7] Turner, broadcasting big-wig and owner of *Cable News Network* (CNN), the *TNT Network*, Chicago's *WTBS-TV* and other media interests, has called Christians "losers" and "Bozos." He is also a bitter critic of America, the nation that has given him so much material wealth and prosperity. Calling the U.S.A. the "big old bully" of world affairs and "the greatest problem in the world," Turner is an ardent supporter of propagandistic New Age world peace projects. A member of the Global Tomorrow Coalition and the Better World Society, Turner's CNN Network has not only produced a six-hour program that depicts the USSR as peace-loving, but he is also a sponsor of the so-called Goodwill Games, a pro-Soviet athletic event.

Joining Turner on the international board of directors of the New Age-oriented Better World Society are such heavyweights as George Arbatov, a high ranking Soviet "public relations" official, Dr. Lester Brown of the ultra-liberal Worldwatch Institute, Gro Harlem Brundtland, prime minister of Norway; Dr. Rodrigo Carazo, President of the University for Peace; Jean Cousteau, the underseas explorer and environmentalist,

Jimmy Carter, former President of the U.S.A., Dr. Julia Henderson, former Secretary General of the International Planned Parenthood Federation; and Olusegun Obasanjo, former head of state of the nation of Nigeria.

U.S. Senator Claiborne Pell. Perhaps the most avid, some would say fanatical, New Ager in the U.S. Congress is Senator Claiborne Pell, Democrat from Rhode Island. Chairman of the powerful Senate Foreign Relations Committee, Pell is a vocal advocate of psychic research on Capitol Hill. According to *U.S. News & World Report*, his bookcase in his private capitol office is crammed with occultic books such as *The Astral* Body, which examines out-of-body experiences. Pell, who admits he frequents spirit mediums, has befriended such New Age notables as psychic magician Uri Geller and the late Theosophy/Hindu philosopher Krishnamurti, who once was thought to be the New Age "christ."[8]

Senator Pell even has a full-time aide, former Naval intelligence officer C. B. Scott Jones, working full-time on "consciousness research." According to Pell, Jones "screens" psychics for him. A tape made by Jones and obtained by *U.S. News & World Report* purportedly contained spirit world conversations with dead newspaper magnate William Randolph Hearst and others.[9]

Sirhan Sirhan. Murderer of U.S. Senator Robert Kennedy and an avowed radical Arab Moslem, Sirhan Sirhan is now incarcerated in Soledad Prison, California. Few realize that Sirhan was a devoted follower of the New Age's Rosicrucian Order (AMORC) at the time he assassinated Kennedy. He had used the Rosicrucian Order's self-hypnosis and visualization techniques to prepare and steel himself for his tragic act of hatred.[10]

Today, Sirhan Sirhan reportedly leads an Alcoholics Anonymous (AA) chapter behind the stone walls of

Soledad. Obviously, his "higher power"--as the AA calls their optional god--is not Jesus Christ.

M. Scott Peck, psychiatrist and author of the #1 bestseller, *The Road Less Traveled*. Peck studied under a Hindu guru in India, practices Zen Buddhist meditation, and conducts New Age-flavored seminars on "Alcohol-The Sacred Disease," "A Taste for Mystery," and "Community and Peace-Making." Peck has written that "God is man's subconscious mind," that the divinity of Jesus is overemphasized, and that man is evolving into godhood. Nevertheless he insists that he is a "Christian."[11] Regrettably, many Christian churches have invited him into their pulpits.

Dr. Jonas Salk. Father of the vaccine that helped to eradicate the polio plague, Dr. Jonas Salk has, in his declining years, increasingly become a promoter of New Age philosophies and schemes. He has also dabbled in the world peace and holistic health movements.[12]

Dr. Robert Muller. Former Assistant Secretary General of the United Nations, all 32 of this organization's agencies and directorate reported to Dr. Muller. Muller is currently Chancellor of the Peace University, a New Age project, and is pushing a Global Core Curriculum he has developed for use in elementary and high schools across America. Muller claims his spirit guide mentor, Djwhal Khul, gave him this curriculum. The curriculum promotes unity of all religions, denigrates Americanism and Christianity, and promotes a one-world government.[13]

Senator Gary Hart. Former U.S. Senator from Colorado and presidential candidate who called for a "New Politics." Senator Hart, who was heartily endorsed in the presidential sweepstakes by other New Age leaders, admits his spiritual advice comes from a Native American Indian "princess" (translated, *witch*).

Barbara Marx Hubbard. Political activist and official with the World Future Society, Barbara Marx Hubbard won the votes of several hundred delegates at the 1984 Democratic Party Convention for the office of Vice President of the United States. One of the most dedicated of New Age leaders, she has repeatedly called for a New World Order. Hubbard has also written that death will be meted out to those who refuse to join their minds to the coming "World Consciousness."[14]

John Randolph Price. Leader of two important New Age groups, the Quartus Foundation and the Planetary Commission. Price, who receives instructions and his marching orders from "Quartus," "Asher" and other demon spirits, is able to marshall thousands of New Age groups, organizations, cults and churches together annually on December 31 to participate in what he calls "World Healing Day." Reportedly, up to 875 million New Age believers from around the globe meditated simultaneously on this same day and moment (12 Noon Greenwich Mean Time). During this extravaganza, Price blasphemously recommended that each affirm "I am the Christ" and decree that "mankind" be transformed into "godkind."[15]

Matthew Fox. Catholic Dominican priest and head of a heretical but popularly received New Age organization called the Center for Creation-Centered Spirituality. Fox has tens of thousands of followers dedicated to abolishing the notion that Jesus is *the* Christ, to bringing in the Aquarian Age, and to worshiping nature. Rev. Fox, who is promoting "Mother Earth" as a living goddess, is an admirer and associate of world famous witch Miriam Starhawk and others involved in witchcraft. He, too, talks with spirit guides from the unseen world.[16]

Edgar Mitchell. Former NASA scientist and astronaut. Mitchell now heads up a New Age organization, the Institute of Homus Noeticus, to promote the New Age "God-man" concept.

James Parks Morton. Pastor of New York City's St. John the Divine Episcopal Church, the largest cathedral in the U.S.A., where such New Age "theologians" as David Spangler, promoter of a "Luciferic Initiation," are frequent speakers. Morton took down the statue of Jesus off the crucifix in his sanctuary and put up a feminine "Christa" in its place. Reportedly, he has also housed a Buddha statue in his church.

Carl Rogers. The late, highly acclaimed psychologist, Rogers was instrumental in revising Catholic School curricula nationwide to include New Age concepts and philosophies.

Richard Bach. Bestselling author of *Jonathan Livingston Seagull, Thinner, One*, and many other novels.

George Lucas. Movie director and producer of the "Star Wars" saga, "Willow," and other New Age-oriented movies. He has teamed up with actor Ron Howard, formerly of *The Andy Griffith Show*, to produce New Age cinemas.

Napoleon Hill. Author of motivational books such as *Think and Grow Rich* that have sold in the millions. Hill wrote that his advisors were a dozen spirit guides, souls of such famous dead men as Thomas Alva Edison and Ralph Waldo Emerson. Hill is big among the success and motivation crowd and among New Age and "Christian" prosperity preachers.

Norman Cousins. Bestselling author and editor. Cousins, president of the World Federalist Society, has stated, "World government is coming. In fact it is inevitable."

Tina Turner. Sultry rock recording artist who admittedly is a big believer in the power of Buddhist chanting.

The Rockefeller Clan. The multimillionaire Rockefeller family is a breeding ground for New Age ideas and programs. At the family mansion in

Tarrytown, New York, Eileen Rockefeller Growold, granddaughter of the late John D. Rockefeller, convenes meetings of the New Age holistic health organization she has founded, the Institute for the Advancement of Health.[17] Meanwhile, David Rockefeller, the influential and rich financier who heads the Chase-Manhattan Bank and sits on the Federal Reserve Bank's Board of Governors, traveled to Colorado in 1987 to help set up a New Age-sponsored World Conservation Bank. It is proposed that all the nations of the world turn over their undeveloped lands to this bank.[18]

Marsha Mason. Actress. A devotee of the late Hindu guru, Baba Muktananda.[19]

Michael Crichton. Best-selling author of *The Andromeda Strain* and director of such movies as *Coma* and *The Great Brain Robbery*, Chrichton's newest non-fiction book, *Travels*, is the story of his New Age and occultic adventures around the globe.[20]

Cher. Actress and singer. At a Halloween party in 1988 at Cher's mansion, guests could get their palms read, auras checked, numerological charts forecast, or Tarot Cards read. Sixteen psychics and thirteen witches attended the gala event.[21]

Phylicia Rashad. Actress who portrays Bill Cosby's wife on the hit TV program, *The Bill Cosby Show*. Rashad, a firm believer in reincarnation and karma, played the starring role as "The Witch" in the occultic Broadway musical, "Into the Woods."

Sharon Gless. Award winning actress of TV's *Cagney and Lacy* policewoman series. Gless is a fanatical supporter of Alcoholics Anonymous' 12-step program, which does not include belief in either Jesus or His Word, nor mention even slightly the concepts of "sin and repentance." Gless told an international TV audience that saw her accept her Emmy Award, "I owe

everything to my best friend, Lazaris." (Lazaris is
Sharon Gless' New Age spirit guide, or demon.)

John G. Fetzer. Multi-millionaire industrialist.
Fetzer is rich, rich, rich! Once the owner of the Detroit
Tigers pro baseball team, he sold the club a few years
ago for the handsome sum of $53 million. All that
money and more--$156 million to be exact--Fetzer has
put into a New Age money trust called the John G.
Fetzer Memorial Fund. He also funded and oversees
the world's leading holistic health and psychic powers
research center, in Kalamazoo, Michigan. The center
is housed in a huge granite building shaped in the form
of a triangle (see Texe's book, *Mystery Mark of the New
Age* to discover the occult meaning of this symbol). At
the very center of the structure stands a huge crystal
rock.

Norman Vincent Peale. World famous minister and
author, and 33rd degree Mason, Peale masquerades as
a positive thinking "Christian." The truth is far
different. Peale encourages astral travel and
communication with the dead, strongly endorsing the
occult book, *The Dead Are Alive: They Can and Do
Communicate With You*, by psychic Harold Sherman.
Peale called Sherman's disgusting book "a
masterpiece!" and gushed "I hope it will be widely
read."[22] Like other New Agers, Peale has called God
an energy force we visualize, one we can breathe in and
out.[23] He also advocated another Jesus and another
gospel (see Galatians 1:8) when he praised the false
New Age Bible, *The Jesus Letters*, written and published
by two Connecticut women, both of whom are spirit
channelers.[24]

Linda Evans. Evans, of TV's *Dynasty* fame, was
once voted "The Most Admired Woman in the U.S.A."
Evans has now moved to Washington state to be with
her New Age spiritual teacher, J. Z. Knight, who
channels the demon spirit "Ramtha." Evans claims that

The Jesus Letters

Edited by Jane Palzere and Anna C. Brown

THE JESUS LETTERS is a small book which were letters received during periods of meditation and inspiration.

We take joy in the following comments from some of our readers:

"What a wonderful gift to all of us from you is your book. THE JESUS LETTERS . . . You will bless many by this truly inspired book."
Dr. Norman Vincent Peale

"Thank you for this incredible book and if you do not mind, I will quote from it often in my lectures."
Dr. Elisabeth Kubler-Ross
Author, Lecturer on Death and Dying

The Jesus Letters is a spirit-channeled New Age book endorsed by Norman Vincent Peale (see back cover above).

Norman Vincent Peale calls this New Age book "a masterpiece!"

Ramtha has totally changed her life and made her aware of the "god-self" she is.

Robert Redford. This veteran actor is active in New Age environmental issues. In 1989, he hosted a symposium on "Global Climate Change" at his resort in Provo Canyon, Utah.[25]

Senator Albert Gore. A democratic party U.S. Senator from Tennessee, Gore has become a popular speaker before New Age groups. In 1989 he co-sponsored a bill in Congress to use tax monies to study New Age and occult methods such as ESP, biofeedback, visualization, transcendental meditation, Zen, yoga, and other forms of Eastern Mysticism. Gore proposed a National Commission on Human Resource Development be created and funded.[26]

Ken Blanchard. Management consultant and bestselling author of *The One Minute Manager*. Blanchard recently was a featured speaker at John Denver's Choices III New Age conference in Aspen, Colorado.[27]

Richard Lamm. Former Governor of Colorado. Lamm made national headlines as governor when he coldly remarked that the elderly need to get out of the way and make way for the young: "You have a duty to die." Winner of the Christian Science Church's Essay for Peace Award, Lamm is a believer in the New Age ecology concept of man's responsibility to be stewards of Mother Earth.[28] This doctrine--of love for Mother Earth while denying the love of Jesus--is being pushed on our youth by the New Age leadership.

Prince Charles. Heir to the crown of Great Britain. Prince Charles has bought into practically every New Age lie imaginable. Among them: the teachings of visualization and occult symbology developed by New Age psychiatrist Carl Jung; ecology; holistic health care and "alternative" medicine; spiritualism, or communication with spirits; psychic miracles; ancient prophecy systems such as the I Ching; astrology; divination by pendulum; and the unity of all religions. The involvement of the Prince and other members of the Royal Family has been detailed in a number of British publications. One of the best researched and documented is the shocking *The Prince and the Paranormal*, a 256-page book published by W. H. Allen and Co. of London.[29]

Obviously, these men and women hold positions of great responsibility. From such highly esteemed vantage places, they wield the power to greatly influence women's minds, change society, to dictate policy in the educational, political, medical, legal, entertainment and social realms. They are often trusted by the masses for their superior intelligence and intellect, their good looks and glamor, or for their leadership ability. Some deny they are "New Agers." A few claim to be Christian but they believe in *another* Christ, *another* Gospel (see Galatians 1; II Corinthians 11:4). Some seek to do good, to serve humanity, but because they have rejected the true Jesus Christ, their hearts and minds are clouded over and polluted. Unwittingly or not, all are servants of Satan, and some work continuously in league with demonic forces, devising new strategies and tactics to bring our children under bondage to the adversary.

Satan has for many years wormed his way into the farthest reaches of our world, planting seeds in the form of demonic-led New Age teachers and leaders--seeds that are even now bearing cruel and evil fruit. Women, beware! Will you place your faith and trust in the rich and famous and in the celebrities and the many powerful men and women of planet earth who now urge you to accept the New Age spirituality? Or instead, will you trust solely in God's Word and in Jesus Christ? This is a question which, soon, every woman alive must decide for herself. There will be no middle ground.

THREE

The Great Sex Carnival: Lust and Abandon in the New Age

Come down, and sit in the dust, O virgin daugther of Babylon, sit on the ground; there is no throne . . . for thou shalt no more be called tender and delicate . . . uncover thy locks, make bare the leg, uncover the thigh. . . . Thy nakedness shall be uncovered, yea thy shame shall be seen . . .

(Isaiah 47:1-3)

Sexuality is sacred because it is a sharing of energy, in passionate surrender to the power of the Goddess, immanent in our desires. In orgasm we share in the force that moves the stars.

Miriam Starhawk
Yoga Journal

Y ou will perceive the true nature of desire," the slick and colorful advertising flyer promises. You will allow the energy of desire to overflow your barriers and sweep you out beyond your separate self into unified ecstasy--functional orgasm. You will receive the fruit of sexual tantra which is to move in the pulsation of life and the energy that is the passion of God."[1]

It was advertised that the sacred sex retreats were to be held on September 23rd, 24th, and 25th, 1988, in Austin, Texas. They were sponsored by One World Life Services (OWLS). The owl is an ancient symbol of the Goddess.

Karen and Charles Glueck, the directors of OWLS, say that their Ascended Master, Father Andre, supposedly a Catholic priest who died hundreds of years ago but is now channeled as Karen's spirit guide, is a specialist at increasing a person's higher consciousness through the release of sexual energy.

Glueck makes this glowing promise to those who attend her spiritual sex retreats:

> You will learn to access your aliveness and sensuality through dance movements, meditation, and ascended breath therapy, supporting your energies and thought blockages, to open up to a free flow of desire in a totality of your being. Desire will become a source of harmony, peace, and innocence in your life. Come with us and enjoy a weekend experience of surrendering to desire.[2]

Unbelievable as it may seem, New Age holy sex seminars, workshops, and retreats are being held across the United State of America and around the world. And enthusiastic students are signing up in droves to attend. For example, one New Age group centered in Pacific Grove, California, recently advertised in major New Age magazines their seminars and workshops called *The Art of Conscious Loving: Spiritualizing Sexuality and Relationships*. Their seminars were held in such cities as Monterey, California; Boston, Massachusetts; Mill Valley, California; New York City; Austin, Texas; Hawaii; San Diego, California; Malibu, California; and Vancouver, British Columbia, Canada.

The ad for these erotic seminars and workshops promised participants that they could increase their energy levels through proper sexual sharing and joining with their spiritual partner. Instructor Charles Muir, explaining that in ancient India, tantric yoga, the art of love, was commonly taught among the Hindus, listed these as the subjects to be taught:

Six methods of male ejaculatory control
Joyful breath release techniques
Celibacy versus tantra
Ritual charging of the chakras through touch
Four types of orgasm
Internal muscular exercises
Kundalini and the chakras
G-spot and other recent discoveries in sexology
Transformative love making
Holy relationship
Energetics of sexual loving
Advanced Eastern techniques of love making
One thousand and one methods of male movement

All of this could be experienced by you during a week-long session for the paltry sum of $395.

New Age Videos and Audiotapes Teach Sacred Sex

Retreats and seminars are not the only places to discover the heights of this shocking New Age ritual. For one thing you can buy a video. In *Yoga Journal* was advertised the video entitled "The Jewel in the Lotus." In the Hindu/New Age theology, the lotus flower symbolizes the female's sex organ and the jewel, the male's. Therefore the "Jewel in the Lotus" is simply a code phrase for *sexual intercourse*. The three video tape set, "The Jewel in the Lotus" was advertised for $209, available from the Kriya Jyoti Tantra Society of California.[3]

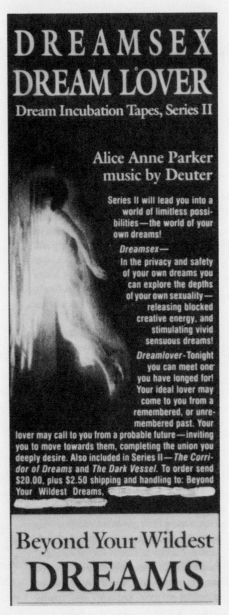

This ad for "Dream Sex" tapes was featured in a number of popular New Age magazines (names and address of company deleted).

In one popular New Age magazine recently appeared an ad for "Dream-Sex" audio cassette tapes. Women were told in the ad that the New Age music on these tapes would assist them in conjuring up, or fantasizing, the "Prince Charming" of their dreams who would then engage in spirit sex with them. In effect, this was a promotion for sexual intercourse with demons known as succubi.

New Age Churches and Cults Provide Sacred Sex Experiences

If, however, you want first hand experience then you may possibly be able to find a sex ritual conducted by a local spiritualist church or join one of a number of New Age cult groups. Sex as a holy ritual is extremely common in such groups.

The New Age cult groups led by Hindu gurus are especially based on either sexual ritual, or simply lustful, uninhibited sex. One woman, now a Christian, who was involved in the New Age for eighteen years before she found Jesus Christ and was released from her bondage, gave me a copy of a prayer she was required to recite three times a day. She stated that sex with her guru was not an unusual occurrence but was all part of living in the ashram. Here is the prayer that she recited. Note that she is appealing to "mother"--in other words, the Mother Goddess:

Oh my mother
I'm in ecstasy
Oh my mother
I am truly in ecstasy

For I have realized my true guru
I found my lord
And my mind is filled
With the song of bliss
Oh my mind dwell forever
High on my sweet lord

Another young lady wrote to us and stated, "For about five years I was much connected with a little known Hindu guru who kept promising his followers 'higher' and 'even higher' initiations. Of course this was tantalizing to us hungry souls who could never seem to reach enlightenment on our own. However it turned out that his highest favors and initiations were sexual."

This young lady stated that she had been a member of the New Age for ten years before she knew the real Christ, Jesus. In her letter to us she remarked that she could "attest mightily to the truths you (Texe) revealed in your book, *Dark Secrets of the New Age*."

Sexual Lies to Women

The New Age movement is capturing tens of thousands of women's souls through sexual lies. Sex, of course, is a big draw throughout our society. Sexual images and erotic fantasies permeate our lives. We cannot turn on our television set or open the pages of a newspaper or a women's magazine without coming face-to-face today with the graphic nature of sexual enticements and inducements. The New Age has mastered the art of inciting lust and unbridled passion in the breast of women.

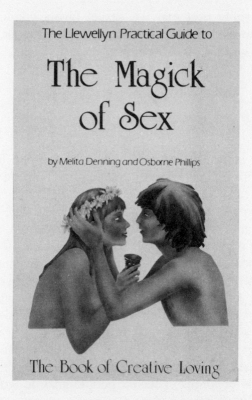

The Llewellyn Practical Guide to

The Magick of Sex

by Melita Denning and Osborne Phillips

The Book of Creative Loving

This popular guide for holy sexual ritual ("magick") is published by a major New Age and occult book company.

It would be difficult to find any area of New Age practice or doctrine that is not somehow related to sexual ritual or a free sex philosophy of some kind. The reason for this is very simple. The New Age *is* Mystery Babylon. This is a religion that has as its core the same unholy practices that were prevalent in Babylon, Egypt, Rome, Greece and throughout the orient. In the centuries before Christ, and in the first centuries after Jesus' first coming, history is replete with the story and descriptions of the fertility rites and the sexual favors granted by the high priestesses in the temples of such cities as Corinth, Athens, Ephesus, and Memphis.[4]

The Great Sex Carnival

The free enjoyment of carnal sex was a prime ingredient of worship in the Mystery religion of Babylon and the Mystery cults of Rome, Greece, and Egypt. Initiates celebrated the sex act with temple prostitutes, many of whom came from the aristocratic class--from the very cream of society. In Ephesus and elsewhere, the cult of Diana encouraged sexual license and sacred promiscuity. The idolatrous statue of Diana depicted her with a multitude of breasts, signifying her sensual nature. In Egypt, the sensual nature of the Mother Goddess, Isis, was also worshipped in fertility rites.

Hislop wrote that Semiramis, the Babylonian "Queen of Heaven," led a licentious life and gave birth to many illegitimate children. Yet, the people grew to worship her as the "Holy Virgin."[5]

In the Goddess religions, it was thought that sacred and ritual sex cleansed and purified; therefore the term "Virgin" was used, though its meaning is obviously far different than that envisioned by Christians. The Roman emperors Nero and Caligula, who professed belief in Roman Gods derived from the Mystery cults of Babylon and Pergamos, were given to sexual orgies and incredible acts of debauchery and sexual depravity. Homosexuality and pederasty (child sex abuse) was rampant throughout the Roman Empire and especially in Greece where the normal practice of heterosexuality (male-female relations) was even sneered at by many of the affluent class and the nobility.

Free Sex in the New Age: A Return to Mystery Babylon

Likewise, the New Age World Religion professes few limits on what is acceptable sexual behavior. Those New Agers who practice tantric yoga actually believe that sexual union--in or out of marriage--brings spiritual communion with the divine energy forces of The Universe. Those involved in witchcraft and Satanism consecrate themselves to Satan through ritual sex orgies.

Marilyn Ferguson, in the New Age classic *The Aquarian Conspiracy*, enthusiastically reports that for many New Agers, sex outside marriage is the wave of the future. She says that the traditional view of fidelity and "one man-one woman" has given way to more "liberated" views. Quoting sociological experts, Ferguson adds that the New Age generation is free from guilt over sex.[6]

Seth, an international network of groups composed of disciples of "Seth," a demon channeled by psychic Jane Roberts, teaches that "the universe is of good intent; evil and destruction does not exist . . . we create our own reality--literally--through the beliefs we hold, and therefore can change what we don't like."[7]

Like most New Age groups, Seth also encourages its believers to enjoy sexual ecstasy outside the bonds of marriage with no fear of retribution. In a recent leaflet published by the Seth Center, the group stated its main ideas regarding sex as follows:

We are in this life to enjoy ourselves-spirit, mind and body. If it isn't fun, stop doing it!. . . . It is natural to be bisexual. Heterosexuality, homosexuality, and lesbianism are equally worthwhile and valid sexual orientations. . . . There is no authority superior to the guidance of a person's inner self.[8]

Miriam Starhawk and her Church of Wicca (witchcraft) no doubt agree with the followers of Seth. Starhawk's views of sexuality exactly parallel the wicked doctrines and fertility ritual of the Babylonian Mystery cults. Among these decadent views is the astonishingly depraved idea that sexual license is godly. Starhawk expresses this view as follows:

> Sexuality is sacred because it is a sharing of energy, in passionate surrender to the power of the Goddess, immanent in our desires. In orgasm we share in the force that moves the stars.[9]

Starhawk teaches that witchcraft is the same as the Goddess religion. "The Goddess," she says, "is the liberator . . . and her service is complete freedom."[10] She also emphasizes, the connection for today's New Age woman with the sexuality of the Goddess:

> The naked body represents truth . . . the law of the Goddess is love: passionate sexual love. . . . The love of the Goddess is unconditional. . . . Any act based on love and pleasure is a ritual of the Goddess. Her worship can take any form and occur anywhere; it requires no liturgy, no cathedrals, no confessions.[11]

As we can see, the New Age lie is that its religion leads to liberty. L. Ron Hubbard, for example, once said that his Scientology, a New Age religion, is "the absolute road to freedom." However, we know from our Bible that the New Age path leads to enslavement. Satan is a liar and the father of lies.

Divine Homosexuality

Liberty, in the New Age view, means that homosexuality and lesbian behavior are perfectly acceptable, even divine. After all, the New Age doctrine of reincarnation holds that a woman alive today could have previously been a man a dozen times or more in past lifetimes. Thus, if a woman is a lesbian, why, it's simply because the vestiges of these past lives remain in her consciousness and are coming to the forefront today.

In the Alice Bailey book, *Esoteric Psychology I*, Djwhal Khul remarks:

> Sex is essentially an expression of . . . unity . . . spirit and matter, male and female, positive and negative; they are in the nature of a stage upon the evolutionary ladder toward a final unity or homo-sexuality . . .

Bailey and other New Age theorists maintain that, eventually, all human beings will evolve into divine beings who incorporate both masculine and feminine features. Bailey says that such persons will be far superior to today's homosexuals. They will be spiritually divine--"true homo-sexuals."

The true New Ager is therefore a true homosexual. Djwhal Khul and Alice Bailey signify the advanced spirituality of such a person by hyphenating the word homosexual (thus, *homo-sexual*).

Radical Feminists Promote Sacred Prostitution

As we've seen, radical feminists in the New Age movement are critical of Christianity and Judaism, alleging that these two faiths are sexist and male-oriented. But the fact is that the gospel of Jesus again and again lifted up women. Heaven is not to be the exclusive province of males. Regardless, some feminists claim that by virtue of women holding high position in the New Age World Religion, this is the only religion for today's women.

History would suggest otherwise. We do have the example of women who, in the Mystery cults of Babylon, served the temples in such high positions as scribes, priestesses, and judges. But the *highest positions* held by women--the position considered the most sacred and holy--were those of *temple harlots and prostitutes*! The Mother Goddess herself was depicted as sensual and erotic, as both sacred and profane, holy yet sexually promiscuous. She was the chief prostitute, the whore whom all other religious women covetously dreamed of imitating.

Is this image of the woman as both priestess and prostitute a desirable one for today's New Age? Evidently so, for we find many New Age feminist writers praising the ancient Goddess cults for their "enlightened understanding" of sexuality. Rita Gross, for example, writes that "the reintroduction today of the image portrayed by sexuality of the goddess represents a basically sane and healthy turn of events." To Gross, the merger of sexuality and spirituality "has much to offer." She announces that the Goddess religion validates women and concludes that "it is good to be in the image of the goddess."[12]

Is it Good to be in the Image of the Goddess?

But what does it mean to say "it is good to be in the image of the goddess?" The disgusting truth is that in the ancient temples where the Babylonian religion was practiced, the males who had sex with the priestesses and

THE GREAT SEX CARNIVAL   □   63

the temple prostitutes believed that they were participating in a "holy marriage ceremony." They believed that they were literally enjoying a supreme act of sexual intercourse with the goddess. They were acting as her bridegroom.

Likewise, the female in the ritual believed that the man's phallus was actually that of a god. In other words, they believed that physical sexual union was accompanied by spiritual union with the divine.[13]

Men, Too, Are Welcomed by the Goddess

We can see, then, the New Age is for men as well. Men are today being told to become more feminine, to let the "feminine side" shine forth and express itself. All this is foolishness, but the majority are falling for it. Psychologists tell them to develop the "right brain"--the "feminine self." The Goddess can then enter the man and become One with him:

> For a man, the Goddess, as well as being the universal life force, is his own, hidden, female self. She embodies all the qualities society teaches him *not* to recognize in himself. She will be the cosmic lover, the gentle nurturer, the eternally desired Other, the Muse, all that he is not. As he becomes more whole and becomes aware of his own "female" qualities . . . he will grow, until he too learns to find Her within.[14]

The New Age Redefines the Term "Virgin"

The pagan Mystery Babylon religions bequeathed to their goddesses the holy title of "Blessed Virgin." But to them, controlled as they were by Lucifer, the word virgin carried an entirely different meaning than the definition in *Webster's Dictionary*. To the pagans, sexual fertility, passion, sensuality, and consummation were synonyms for virginity. The virgin was one who gave sexual favors to all, but was controlled by no man. The same is true in today's New Age theology, in which women are encouraged to transform themselves into "sacred prostitutes."

In her new book, *The Sacred Prostitute*, Nancy Qualls-Corbett explains how the modern New Age Movement has adopted the pagan definitions and meanings. She writes:

> The Goddess was considered virginal . . . the virginal attribute of the Goddess simply means she belongs to no man, rather she belongs to herself. . . . The Goddess of Love exists in her own right as 'one-in-herself.'

> The woman (of today) who comes to know the Goddess grows in the understanding of that divine aspect of her feminine nature. . . . For example she finds her body beautiful . . . cares for her body with proper nutrition and exercise and enjoys the ceremonies of bathing, cosmetics, and dress . . .

> The woman who accepts her physcial and psychological feminity lives in harmony with the sacred prostitue within. She serves the Goddess of Love by attending the holy fire of her inner feeling. . . . The ego then acknowledges a higher authority, the self.[15]

New Age woman is, therefore, what rock star Madonna calls the "Material Woman"--self-centered, full of self-love, arrogantly prideful, witchy, and defiantly sexual. Is it any woder that one of Madonna's hit songs is entitled "Like A Virgin!"

Orgies and Sacred Sex to Wash Away Sin

Virgin is not the only word given a radically new meaning by the New Age. As we have seen, the sexual ritual in a temple was one way in which the New Age pagans of yesteryear confused fleshly desires with spiritual attainment. In many cities orgies were routinely held as part of religious festivals. To Christians this is no doubt a revolting thing and evidence of just how far Satan can twist the human soul. However, the worshippers of the Mother Goddess believed that it was through sexual union that a person's mind and soul was cleaned and purified. Sex was considered a form of baptism. It was a ritual, explained one historian, that "washed away sin."

This same meaning is applied by the New Age today. What this means, then, is that it doesn't matter who you have sex with, or when or where you have sex, and it doesn't matter if you are married to your sexual partner or not, the only thing that matters is this: do you consider sexual intercourse a *holy ritual*, a *sacred art*? If so, then the sex act, the New Age teaches, is lifted from the profane to higher levels of sublime spirituality.

The ancient notion that in the act of holy sex the two individuals were actually achieving sexual union with the god (or gods) is highly recommended by many of today's New Age teachers. Matthew Fox, for example, in his book *Original Blessing*, quotes medieval mystic Meister Eckhart as describing God as "voluptuous and delicious." In applying his sick reasoning, Fox proclaims:

> Ours is truly an erotic god. Does not God the Mother play? What kind of mother would it be who never played with her babies? Does not God the lover play? What kind of lovers would they be who did not play together?[16]

Achieving Higher Consciousness Through Sex

Prominent New Age teachers tell their followers that the sexual experience "is at the core of all mystical experience."[17]   For example, two New Age scholars, Monica Sjoo and Barbara Mor, write, "The first religion, originated by women, was a sexual-spiritual religion, the celebration of cosmic ecstasy."[18]   They also explain that, "tantra sex proclaims that all things . . . are the active play of the female creative principle: the Goddess of many forms, sexually penetrated by an invisible, indescribable, seminal male."   They then go on to recommend, "prolonged acts of ecstatic meditation in sexual union with a partner."[19]

Sjoo and Mor also say that "liturgies, mantras, intervisualizations, yoga postures, and manipulation of the joined female and male energies" can heighten the ecstatic spiritual experience.[20]

The Moon Goddess, Sjoo and Mor note, "was worshipped in orgiastic rites, being free to take as many lovers as she chose. Women could surrender themselves to the goddess by making love to a stranger in her temple. This has been called . . . sacred prostitution."[21]

Holy, Ritual Sex--A Necessity of the Last Days Religion of the Beast

We should not be surprised that holy, ritual sex is part of the New Age. If the New Age is truly Mystery Babylon, then this is a world-wide religion that will bring back *all* the ungodly practices and bizarre behavior of the Babylonian religion. The New Age World Religion certainly does this. Sexual perversions are accepted as legitimate   lifestyles in the New Age.   Bisexuality, lesbianism, homosexuality, transvestitism, incest--it does not matter what your perverse sexual tastes are. The New Age approves. After all, the New Age contends that each of us is a god. And as a god or a goddess we can choose the sexual path to godhood that we most prefer.

It should be remembered that in many of the areas where the Goddess was worshipped, incestual relations between mother and son, brothers and sisters, and fathers and daughters, was considered normal and even desirable for the human deities--the gods and the goddesses in the heavenly realms. Promiscuity among the worshippers of the Goddess was sometimes regarded as a divine service and a responsibility. Even bestiality was accepted by many.[22]

In Babylon it was said that the goddess Ishtar could become angry and violent if a man refused to have sex with her. For example, in the Babylonian manuscript, *The Epic of Gilgamesh*, the goddess Ishtar is infuriated when King Gilgamesh refuses to have sex relations with her. Venting her anger, she threatens to release the dead from the invisible nether world so that they will outnumber the living.

In Egypt the goddess Hathor was the mistress of sexual pleasure, alcoholic drinks and inebriation. She was the goddess women turned to for dance, music and song. Her admirers called her the "mistress of the vulva" and of love. Through prayers and offerings to her it was believed that this goddess could help a woman by stimulating her sexuality and fertility.

Hathor was also known as the tree goddess. In the *Egyptian Book of the Dead*, the dead sat under Hathor's tree to keep her company and seek renewal. This is one reason today why witches believe that trees are very sacred, living creatures that connect with the earth and should be respected and venerated.

Occult expert Robert Anton Wilson relates to us this ancient New Age doctrine of sacred sex. He writes that

Nuit, the female Egyptian divinity of the stars, invited her children with veiled sexual metaphors as follows:

> I love you! I yearn to you! . . . Put on the wings, and arise the coiled splendor within you: *Come unto me!*[23]

Sex and the Awakened New Age Goddess

Most New Agers who emphasize the return and the awakening of the Goddess are delighted that sexuality is once again moving to center stage of society and religion. Rita Gross, in *The Book of the Goddess*, urges women to consider the Hindu female deities as a resource "for the contemporary rediscovery of the goddess." She says that "the reintroduction of the goddess . . . represents a basically sane and healthy turn of events." According to Gross, "sexuality and spirituality has much to offer."[24]

The New Agers who specialize in occultism have also jumped on the sexual bandwagon. David Wood, a man who has done much research on the occult system called the "Quest for the Grail," writes that the satanic symbol of the pentagram actually is identified sexually with the female body. The female body has five openings, he notes, just as the pentagram has five points. He further writes that the pentagram, the "blazing star," was associated with the goddess Venus, who was fondly called the Goddess of Love.[25]

Witches, too, join their fellow New Agers in promoting sacred sex. Irena Tweedie, a well known witch, states in her diary, *The Chasm of Fire*, that "sexual energy is extremely important." Without sexual energy, she says, "a person can never realize the Self."[26]

The *Self* you will recall, is a word used by the New Age to indicate the realization of the god or goddess within.

In fact, to realize the Self (also called the Higher Self) is actually to become demon possessed. So what Tweedie is saying is that without the release of sexual energy and inhibitions a woman will never become incarnated by the Goddess. She will never experience God within.

It should also be understood that the *unicorn*, a very popular symbol in the New Age, is a mythical beast that is accorded a sexual role by the occult. In the ancient occultic myth, the unicorn, representing the moon, dances to and fro sidestepping the *solar lion* who seeks to take away the unicorn's virginity. Finally though, the horn of the unicorn gets stuck fast in a tree. The lion then swiftly moves in for the assault. Another occult piece of lore is that the unicorn can only be captured by a human virgin.

Sex Fever in the New Age

The sexual theme grows more important for the New Age each day. Women are encouraged to take the lead in this so called "spiritual sexual revolution." A New Ager who is also a Catholic nun, Sister Madonna Kolbenschlag, at a recent Christian woman's conference, stated:

> Women are clearly the catalyst for the formation of the new spirituality. It is women above all who are in the process of reversing Genesis . . . by validating and freeing their sexuality. . . . Why should we be surprised that the Holy One is breaking through the consciousness of humanity as the Goddess . . .[27]

"Women," said Kolbenschlag, "must manifest their 'full desire for godlikeness.'" Otherwise, "they will be left behind in Egypt while we journey to the promised land and the new covenant." "Women today," she urged, "must reclaim their reality . . . through the power of a holistic sexuality, and the right to a free and personally responsible expression of it."[28]

Kolbenschlag also enthusiastically remarked that, "women have always experienced the inner connection of sexuality, affectivity, religious zeal and the creative impulse." "And so," she said, "we have to ignore the Great Lie that denies this."[29]

The Great Lie, as Kolbenschlag terms it, is (in the New Age view) God's Word, the Bible. Holy and sacred sex is Satan's idea and he no doubt delights in branding the morality of God a "Great Lie."

It is thought by New Age theologians that by experiencing their sexuality women will help the entire earth to more rapidly become a New Age Kingdom. Through sexual prowess and experience there will be developed a new Cosmic Consciousness. David Spangler calls this *planetary spirituality*.[30]

The Lucis Trust and the Doctrine of Sexual Energy

It would be unusual if the Lucis Trust, perhaps the most effective New Age organization in existence today in terms of propagandizing the New Age message around the world, was not involved in promoting the new sexual philosophies and practices of the New Age. Indeed, the Lucis Trust has published a book, *A Compilation on Sex*, supposedly dictated to Alice Bailey, the organization's founder, by her spirit guide, Djwahl Khul, which summarizes the Lucis Trust's doctrines of holy sex. In this revealing guide to New Age sexuality, Bailey states that:

> Sex . . . is lifted up into the light of day in order that man may reach complete union with divinity. Man discovers

that sex (which has hitherto been a purely physical
function, carried on sometimes under the impulse of love)
is elevated into its rightful plane as the divine marriage.[31]

Alice Bailey claims that "cosmicly speaking, it (sex)
manifests as the attractive force between spirit and
matter."[32] Moreover, in her book, *Ponder on This*, Bailey,
again inspired by her spirit guide Djwhal Khul, remarks:
"out of the many sexual experiments now going on, the
coming generation . . . will tip the scales in a desired di-
rection . . . sex will be seen eventually to be a proper and
divine function."[33]

Alice Bailey goes on to make the mind boggling
assertion that it is through divine sexual energy now
streaming out from the "Holy Center" that the New Age
kingdom will be brought to reality. Sexual rites evidently
are a prime ingredient in the initiations planned by the
New Age for all humanity, except of course for the
"inferior" fundamentalist Christian race.

It is the will of god to produce certain radical and
momentous changes in the consciousness of the race,
which will completely alter man's attitude to life. . . . It is
this course which will bring about that tremendous crisis,
the initiation of the race into the Mystery of the Ages, into
that which has been hid from the beginning.[34]

The Holy Sex Ritual as the Cornerstone of the Coming One World Religion

God has made woman and man with the innate capacity to
enjoy sex as a healthy and enriching experience. But as
we have learned, Satan has sought to destroy the beauty
and wondrous nature of sexuality by infusing his

perversions and practices. There are very few New Age authorities today who have not jumped on the bandwagon and begun to promote the revival of sacred, or holy, sex.

I am not speaking of only the New Age theologians, occultists, feminists, and lovers of ancient Babylon and Egypt. No, the best and the brightest of the New Age are bringing in a new theology based on sex as spirituality. Mystery Babylon has returned with a vividness and imaginative creativity that should shock each one of us.

An example is M. Scott Peck, the medical doctor and psychiatrist whose book *The Road Less Traveled* and others have sold in the millions. Peck has gone on the road giving seminars and conferences on the topic "Sexuality and Spirituality: Kissing Cousins." Like other New Age leaders, Peck teaches that the intimate relationship between sexuality and spirituality so well known to the mystics is now to be given "to a public eager for the knowledge." "This," says Peck, "is both exciting and healing."[35]

Meanwhile, Chris Griscom, a popular teacher with the Light Institute in New Mexico has published a new book entitled *Ecstasy is a New Frequency*. Griscom says that the sexual spirituality movement of the New Age actually began in the 60s and 70s but has achieved new levels of consciousness throughout the decade of the 80s.[36] "To practice holy ritual sex," Griscom comments, "is to exercise our godhood. Sexual ecstasy," she states, "is the Higher Self in action."[37]

Again, you will recall that the term Higher Self, for the New Ager, means the god within every person. The discerning Christian recognizes this as a code phrase for *demonic control*.

According to Griscom, when we enjoy a sexual encounter and achieve orgasm we become one with the universal spirit:

The unmanifest, which is spirit, funnels in on that which takes form, such as in the sexual, genital area.[38]

The New Age Promotion of Immorality

So what does all of this mean for you and me? First of all we see that the New Age is one of the greatest promoters today of sexual immorality. There can be little doubt that the gay rights movement, for example, has been one of the major goals of the New Age leadership. Likewise, sex education in the classroom, as it is taught today, also has long been a New Age goal. Unrestrained sex has resulted in the loss of innocence for millions of young girls. This too, has been a primary New Age goal over the last few decades.

The sexual immorality that has been brought into society by the New Age should be most alarming to us. However, this is only a symptom of a deeper-seated problem. I am convinced that it is through the newly introduced doctrine of *sacred sex* that the New Age, in years to come, will attempt to entice and lure thousands of new recruits and converts. By claiming that sex is holy and that, if practiced as a spiritual exercise, sex can literally catapult a woman to godhood and divinity, the New Age leadership has proven its ability to project itself to the forefront of "new" religious trends. For we who know Jesus Christ and understand the signs of the times, this is not so new after all. The revival of the Babylonian doctrine of sacred and holy sex is proof positive that we are in the last days. Mystery Babylon is now taking its final shape. The sensual religion prophesied to return in the last days is here.

FOUR

The Unholy Trinity: Father of Light, Bride of Darkness, and Son of Perdition

Let no man deceive you by any means: for that day (the coming of the Lord) shall not come, except there come a falling away first, and that man of sin be revealed, the son of perdition; Who opposeth and exalteth himself above all that is called God, or that is worshipped; so that he as God sitteth in the temple of God, showing himself that he is God.

(II Thessalonians 2:3-4)

In all that was Holy, was Satan.

David Wood
Genesis: The First Book of Revelation

Does Satan have a wife? Or, considering his ungodly character, perhaps the question should be phrased: Does Satan have a *mistress*? Is there a Mother Goddess of the New Age--the Mystery Woman of Sin--identified in the Bible as the Mistress of Satan?

The Mother of the Beast

Bible prophecy provides us with the astonishing fact that Satan does indeed have a mistress--a spiritual mistress. She is described as the *harlot*, a supremely evil and deadly Mystery Woman of Sin. To her can be attributed the black credit of all the blood of the martyred saints which has ever been shed. I, therefore, call her the *Bride of Darkness*. Revelation 17 prophesies her glorious rise, her majestic reign, and her hideously tragic, ultimate destiny --her flesh will be eaten and her remains burned with fire!

The Father of Lies

We know also that in the Bible, Jesus identifies the one who is behind all the combined evils of the world as Satan, "who is a liar and the father of it." He was, said Christ, a "murderer from the beginning" (John 8:44). Satan is also found in Bible prophecy. In Revelation 12:9, he is called "the great dragon . . . that old serpent, the Devil, and Satan, which deceiveth the whole world."

And These Two Shall Conceive A Son!

God's Word also reveals to us that Satan and his Mistress, the Woman of Sin, the Whore of Mystery Babylon, will conceive a *son*. This unholy offspring will be raised to be just as hellish as his father. He will, so to speak, be a chip off the old block. Indeed, he will be the very incarnation in the flesh of his spiritual father, Satan. Revelation 13 describes him as the Beast, the man whose number is 666.

The apostle Paul unveils him as the *son* of the devil: the "son of perdition" (II Thessalonians 2). The pagans called him the "fruit of the womb" of the woman.

The birth of a "son" by the "Mother Goddess" is Satan's atrocious masquerade of creating the false Christ prophesied by the Bible. New Age believers are falling for this lie because they are under a great delusion. Most do not recognize that the New Age is to bring forth the Antichrist into power, even though their leadership does little to disguise the awful truth. Here for example is how one top New Ager describes the birth and tutoring of the one whom Christians will recognize as the coming "son of perdition:"

> She is the Great Mother who gives birth to him as the Divine Child Sun. . . . She is the Initiatrix who teaches him the Mysteries. He is the young bull; she is the nymph, seductress. . . . He is the Lord of Death.[1]

From Babylon.

From India.

The Mother Goddess was said to have given birth to a son. Pictured above are representations of idols from Babylon and India depicting the Mother Goddess and Son.

The Rise and Fall of the Trinity of the Damned

It is remarkable that in one single book of prophecy alone, the three entities of the Unholy Trinity of the Damned are mentioned and their fates revealed. *Revelation* is that magnificent book. In it, we find the images, descriptions, and destiny of Satan (Revelation 12:9 and 20:10), his mythical Mistress (Revelation 17) and their son (Revelation 13 and 20:10).

Satan himself, Revelation explains, will eventually destroy his worldwide religious system of false gods and goddesses built upon the common altar of the Mother Goddess of Babylon image (Revelation 17:16-17). But later, he himself must face the verdict and wrath of Almighty God. Here is what is to come regarding the devil and his son, the beast:

And the devil that deceived them was cast into the lake of fire and brimstone, where the beast and the false prophet are, and shall be tormented day and night, forever and ever (Revelation 20:10).

Also dim is the fate of those men and women who reject Jesus and instead allow themselves to be seduced by the unholy trinity of the New Age. The Bible tells us that they, too, will be judged for their disobedience. They, too, will drink of the wrath of the Lord and be cast into hell (Revelation 14:9-10). This is, of course, a fate in which today's New Age believers refuse to believe. But every prophecy of the Bible has come to pass and so shall this one.

The Goddess is Alive! Magick is Afoot!

Many, many New Agers believe that the Mother Goddess exists. Many refer to the concept of *archetypes*, first developed by occult psychiatrist Carl Jung. According to Jungian psychology and theory, embraced by the New Age leadership, you and I are co-creators of this earth. As co-creators we have supposedly invented all of the gods and goddesses (archetypes) who have ever been honored and decorated with our own minds. According to this theory, thoughts take form in the spirit world first, then later, manifest in the physical world as reality. Therefore, this New Age psychology doctrine proposes that the Mystery Babylon Goddess, as well as the other goddesses and gods of the pagans, were created when men began to think of them, imagine their existence, and worship them. Thus, *they became real.* The ancient Mother Goddess, then, is a *myth* that is, at the same time, *real.*

We understand, then, also why C. S. Lewis can profess that Jesus is the fulfillment of *myth*, yet simultaneously insist that Jesus was the myth that became real.[2]

This is why such New Age leaders of today, such as Diane Stein, can trumpet aloud the pronouncement that "The Goddess is Alive: Magick is Afoot! Women everywhere are discovering the Goddess, learning where she came from and what she means for them."[3]

The New Age is not new. It is simply the old goddess religions of Babylon, Egypt, India, Rome, Canaan, Greece, Gaul, and Britain, in new, 20th century packaging. As one New Age authority explains:

> You create your own reality. . . . In the New Age of
> metaphysics and spirituality, this creation occurs in the
> conscious mind. The New Age . . . is a state of mind.

People have been discovering their own New Age for thousands of years. . . . It is just that many, many more are making their personal discovery *now*.[4]

Satan's Fertile Imagination Created the New Age Goddess

The truth however, as the Bible reveals, is that we are not co-creators.   God is the sole creator of this universe, of the spirit as well as the physical realms (Colossians 1:15-19.   Thus, man did not create his own god, goddesses, and gods.   Where then did this visionary figure of the Mother Goddess come from?   Quite simply, she comes from the fertile imagination of Satan.   She is not real at all, but is an imaginary fantasy figure.   That she does indeed manifest in the minds of New Age women and men and possibly exist physically may well be the case.   For Paul tells us that Satan's angels can come as angels of light. They may disguise themselves in any form they wish.   The ultimate reality, however, is that in whatever form the Goddess takes, however she "reaches out and touches someone," she is simply a demonic entity, an imaginary creation of the devil.

Moreover, the devil created the goddess image simply as a trap to lure and induce men to sample her wares and entrance, enchant, and captivate women to become seduced by her beauty, charm, and nurturing characteristics. Of course it is true that no one that knows Jesus Christ as Lord sees anything in the Goddess other than the blackness of hell.   Any true believer can recognize the myth of the Goddess as a hellish scam. As I have proven, the New Age believer, as well as those who have rejected Jesus Christ and His Truth, have opened themselves up to the *strong delusion* so that they *will believe* a lie (II Thessalonians 2).

White Light Pentacles/Sacred Spirit Products
"TRADITIONAL MAGICKS FOR THE NEW AEON"

A well-known witchcraft newspaper carried this illustration (top) of the Goddess and her master, the Horned God (Lucifer). The cupid-like angel is their Son. Below is an ad offering "magick" products for the "New Aeon" (New Age).

It is not surprising that Satan would choose for himself an imaginary goddess. This allows him to present the fictitious myth that he is both our Father and our Mother. It also gives him one additional avenue in which to work his diabolical will. Satan can also claim to be a Trinity. His offspring, the man-child of the unholy affair of the Goddess and Satan, is a *Son*. Not an ordinary son; no this is the Son of Perdition, the Antichrist, also described as the Beast (see Revelation 13 and II Thessalonians 2).

Osiris seated on his throne.
From the Papyrus of Nesi-ta-neb-ashru.

EGYPTIAN

RELIGION

In this ancient popyrus drawing we discover the unholy trinity of the Egyptian goddess religion. Seated is Osiris the horned father god. Behind him is the goddess Isis, and their son, Horus. The snake is the focus of this trinity; the woman (Goddess) is therefore depicted with the head of a serpent and destroyer weapons in her hands.

Through his New Age teachers Satan has spread the false teachings of his Father-Mother God doctrine. Thus, a demonic entity that came to one prominent New Age leader reportedly declared:

I am father. I am mother. I am Heaven. I am Earth. I wait to be united. I long to be united. I am whole only with my wife of Earth. I am full only with my husband of Heaven.

Where are our children to unite us? Oh sons and daughters of all of Earth we beseech you. Call unto Us, your Heavenly Father and Earthly Mother, and we will complete your life. Unite Us within you, and you will be Full of All Living Power.[5]

The New Age myth, unbelievable as it may sound, is that the Father God, Satan (also called Sanat), is represented by and even is the *sun* that radiates its rays in our planetary region. The Goddess is represented by our earth. The Sun is also called, simply, heaven. Therefore, when heaven and earth are wed, when they are united and made one, they can then someday produce together an offspring, the *Son*, whom Christians know through Bible prophecy will be the Beast, the Antichrist. This belief is at the core of what occultists call "The Secret Doctrine."

The Unholy Trinity of the New Age

What we have, then is the Unholy Trinity of Satan: Father, Mother, Son. Occultists call their god Lucifer the "Father of Light." Again we recall that Paul warned us that Satan and his demons come disguised as "angels of light" (II Corinthians 11:12-15). Moreover, throughout

the ages, the false religions of the "New Age" invariably
worshipped the Sun God and his mistress. Like many in
today's New Age they, too, adored the being known as the
"Father of Light." David Spangler, a top New Ager of
today writes:

> The light that reveals to us the path to (the New Age)
> Christ comes from Lucifer. He is the light giver. . . . It is
> his light that heralds for man the dawn of a greater
> consciousness. . . . The true light of this great being can
> only be recognized when one's own eyes see with . . . the
> light of the inner sun. . . . It is an invitation into the New
> Age.[6]

As we have discovered, this unholy "Father of Light"
has a mate or mistress, whom we can accurately identify as
his "Bride of Darkness." A son is soon to be conceived--a
false Christ in fleshly form.

Now the terrible aspect of this unholy trinity of Satan
is that just as the real God calls us to be sons and
daughters--just as Jesus invited us to reside in Him and
He in us--Satan calls forth every woman and man on earth
to be *whole in he and his goddess*.

The Two Brides

Again we see the reality of *two* brides. You can become
part of either bride. One bride is the holy and chaste
bride of Christ Jesus; the other bride belongs to Satan.
Deceptively, Satan also calls his bride, composed of all
those women and men on earth who worship and who
have rejected Jesus Christ, a *virgin bride*. The word virgin
takes on a horrendously different meaning when used by
Satan's New Age occultists. A virgin in occultic terms is

one who has become possessed or is controlled by the demonic forces. Obviously this is a complete reversal of what the Bible means by the same term, virgin.

You should know that if you are not a child of God, then the devil can do with you whatever he desires. As horrifying as it is, you are the child of the devil. This is why in one popular New Age magazine, the New Age god (Lucifer) and his mistress (the mythical Goddess) call on men and women everywhere to unite with them:

> Our power is experienced through the wedding of Heaven and Earth. Our love is encouraged through our children awakening to each of Us within them. We give to you, oh beautiful sons and daughters of earth, your inheritance. You are children of Heaven and children of Earth, and children of night you shall be no more, for the morning of the wedding feast has begun.

> We are witnessing a precious moment in earth's history. The union of the Heavenly Father and Mother Earth. It is the wedding feast of eternal light, where the Spiritual Power of Heaven connects with and joins the physical power of earth.

> This union can only take place within the embodied forms of their children--the children of Light. As we integrate Spirit with Earth, male and female, we create the wedding feast--the New Age.[7]

Above we see Satan's attempt to counterfeit the wedding feast of the Lamb. Can there be any doubt whatsoever that Satan is the master counterfeiter of all time! He comes as the Father of Light but is darkness personified. In the following chapter we will shed more real light--from above--on that darkness as we unmask Satan's strategy to win the minds of women today.

FIVE

Unmasking the Hidden Darkness

"They forgot God their Savior, which had done great things. . . . They joined themselves also unto Baal."
(Psalm 106:18-21, 28)

"We are one. It is overwhelming. I kissed her and we left our physical bodies. . . . We merged our flames. We are in God, in each other, and in the earth."

"Bob"
Gabriel's Horn Magazine

I felt a tingle in my spine. Then this overpowering light flashed in my head like the sun. I was overcome with euphoria and ecstasy. I'll never forget that light!"

This is how one woman described the moment when she received her *transformation* as a "born again" New Ager. Satan does indeed come as an angel of light. He has long been symbolized by the fiery sun--the most intense and chaotic light in our galaxy. All the pagan deities were known as gods of light--representatives of the great Sun God, the Father of Light, Lucifer.

Let us therefore see if we can go beyond the glaring bright light that is Satan's facade and expose the massive vacuum of darkness that lies hidden behind the blinding first flash. It is important we recognize that the Adversary is uniting woman after woman today with he and his false goddess. What are some of his tactics?

Uniting With the False "Gods" of Light--The Holy Sex Act

Satan has concocted an elaborate scheme to recruit people in service to he and his goddess. One major way this can be accomplished is through a *sacred sex act*. In an earlier chapter I covered the subject of what New Agers term *holy sex* or *tantric sex* in great detail. But it is important here to re-state the essential facts about this deception. The New Age teaches that when a man and a woman enter into an act of sexual intercourse an energy field is established which connects that man and woman with the god and goddess. Moreover, it is taught that in the sex act, and especially as ecstasy and orgasm are achieved, the man and woman become One with each other and also One with the androgynous God, who is a unified Father of Light (Satan) and Goddess, or Bride, of Darkness.

This is how one couple described their induction through holy sex into an ungodly union with Satan and his Mistress: This is the story of Bob and Linda, as told first by Bob:

> I have had some very deep experiences . . . I've had that wonderful feeling of complete connectiveness . . . between myself and God. But I have never experienced the male and female aspect of God coming together that, in my first meeting with Linda I experienced.

We are one. It is overwhelming. I kissed her and we left our physical bodies and we were in a body that was more familiar to us. A history of lives rushed at me.

We merged our flames. We are in God, in each other, and in the earth."[1]

Linda, the female partner of this New Age duo, is quoted as saying:

I'm pregnant. Bob found me this way. Perhaps others would criticize us and say that this baby is another man's, but this baby is love's baby. She belongs to the planet. We do not own her . . . she is a child of Light and God is her Father. We will all love her and do our best to do what is right for her.

Bob is such a strong part of my life . . . when I was first 'touched' by him, I felt flames come out of the top of my head and my body felt vast. There was an aliveness in me and I was aware of a whole new set of (Hindu) chakras; there was a holiness about being together with him. I know bliss! I am alive! I feel myself as a powerful woman . . . ready to do the spiritual thing that I came to this planet to do.[2]

From the story of Bob and Linda, as told in their own words, we can certainly see all the signs of a strong delusion. Bob admits that he and Linda engaged in sexual intercourse the very first time they met. Each profess that it was an intense spiritual connection. Bob even explained that he felt that they left their physical bodies in an out-of-the-body experience. Note also the mention of flames and the fact that Linda experienced a heightened sense of power.

It is also significant to note that Linda, the woman involved in this instance, has no moral problem with what she is doing. Although she is pregnant by another man when she meets Bob, she contends that this, too, is a positive spiritual thing. Rather than taking responsibility for the new life that she helped to bring in this world, she detaches herself spiritually and emotionally from the baby by pretending "this baby is love's baby. She belongs to the planet. We do not own her. She is a child of Light and God is her father." In a sense, Linda has given her baby over to the devil, for he is, in occultic terms, always called the Father of Light.

Keep in mind too, that when Linda calls her love child, impregnated in her through illicit sex, the child of her "god," the Father of Light, she is making a claim that this is a holy child conceived in a manner similar to the way in which Mary conceived baby Jesus. Such faulty reasoning is why Satan's New Age has been able to convince so many thousands of women that illicit affairs can be healthy and good. It also explains how Satan can abuse the term "virgin," for virgin to Satan simply means a woman who is faithful to *him* in her emotions, spiritual actions, and fleshly activities.

It is sad that the New Age is grooming thousands of young women today to become bearers of "Rosemary's Baby." Conceived in sin, these babies often are coming into the world with the unfortunate circumstances that they will be raised as little New Agers from their earliest breath. This is the ultimate horror and it is why Texe wrote his expose' of Satan's plan to destroy our children.

Sunlight (Father) Impregnates the Earth (Mother)

Just as the New Age hopes to inspire so many women to consider the sexual act, in or out of marriage, as a compact and a union with Satan as the Father of Light, its teachers seek to provide a planetary connection between the devil and his mistress. Exalting nature, New Age teachers propose that the Sun, representing the father, and the Earth, representing the mother, are intimately joined through a *celestial sex act:*

> Sunlight impregnates the earth. Solar sperm and ocean ovum mingle. The sun teaches the earth his song, and the earth teaches the sun hers. The sun tries to sing her song and laughs. And the earth tries to sing a sun song and creates blue sky, white clouds, and a world of scurrying creatures below.[3]

These symbols of the sun as a deity all came from New Age publications. Lucifer is, in reality, the great Sun God of the New Age.

The New Age Mystery Babylon religion has restored the ancient doctrine of the Solar Spirit, the fire god, the sun, who was worshiped by many names and under many guises by the ancients. In Egypt, he was Osiris, in Babylonia, Marduk and Baal. In Rome the god Saturn was the Great Sun God and in Greece he was known as Apollo. In today's New Age, such groups as the Lucis Trust have identified the Hindu god, Lord Agni, as their "Lord of Fire."

This fire god of the pagans always had a mistress. We note that in the astrology of the mythologies, Virgo the woman, the "celestial virgin" and "sacred prostitute," was pictured as bearing a branch of fruit in her arms. This branch of fruit represented the son to come.

This occultic doctrine of the Sun God impregnating divine Mother Earth, his Goddess, has even been widely spread throughout the Christian world. Its source has been the devotional book *God Calling*, supposedly written by "two anonymous women," but actually dictated to them by a lying spirit calling itself "God." This demonic spirit endorses the New Age doctrines that Mother Earth is the Goddess:

Nature is the embodied spirit of my thoughts. . . . Treat Her as such . . . as truly my servant and messenger (March 8 devotional).

Earth gave me her best--a human temple to enclose my Divinity, and I brought her the possession of Divine Power, Divine Love, Divine Strength" (August 19 devotional).[4]

Unbelievable as it may seem, *God Calling*, a book written by demons, has been called a "Christian Classic" and is currently on the top ten Christian Bestseller List!

The Trail Leads to Satan

All paths lead to God, say New Age teachers. This is diametrically opposite to what the Bible teaches. The Scriptures testify that all paths, except the path to Jesus Christ, lead to destruction. It is important to keep in mind that every time a New Ager or occultist uses the term "God" they are referring to *their god*, Lucifer. Lucifer, or Satan, is the inventor of the Mystery Babylonian religion. As occultist David Wood writes in *Genesis: The First Book of Revelations*, "In all that was Holy, was Satan."[5] Wood notes that Madam Blavatsky, founder of Theosophy, revealed the very same thing in her book *Isis Unveiled*. On page 13 of this occult book, Blavatsky revealed that this "Supreme Deity" is also known as "the central, spiritual sun."

G. H. Pember, in a scholarly work on the mysteries, *Earth's Earliest Ages*, explains that this supreme deity, under the name *Satan*, is the Sun God of pagan times. He also affirms that Satan was the object of veneration by those who practiced the Mystery Religions:

> There is little doubt that the culmination of the mysteries was the worship of Satan himself.[6]

Although Satan was the ultimate object of worship in the Mystery Religions, his mate and mistress, the Goddess, also enjoyed a high place of honor just as she does today in the modern New Age movement. Together they provide us an unexcelled picture of a hellish duo, two soul twins destined for perdition, he the serpent, she the mythical spirit of the universe. As Joseph Campbell, the late New Age philosopher, relates in *Occidental Mythology:*

> In the mystery cults . . . the place of honor was held . . . by a
> goddess, darkly ominous, who . . . was the mother of both
> the living and the dead. Her consort was typically in
> serpent form; and her rites were . . . characterized . . . in
> spirit dark and full of dread. The offerings were . . . of pigs
> and human beings, directed downward, not upward to the
> light, and rendered . . . in twilight groves and fields, over
> trenches through which the fresh blood poured into the
> bottomless abyss.[7]

The Goddess then, is she who demanded sacrifice, the
sacrifice of human blood. The early gnostics called her
Sophia, claiming that the Goddess was the Intelligence of
the Universe, the Universal Spirit, the Word. This too, is
evidence of another satanic counterfeit. What we are
seeing then in this unholy combination is that Satan, as
the Father of Light, counterfeits God; and his mistress,
the Goddess, counterfeits the Holy Spirit. Meanwhile,
the one to come, the Antichrist, counterfeits Jesus, the
Son.

It is interesting to note that in her book *When
Humanity Comes of Age*, noted New Age theologian,
Britain's Vera Alder, contends that the Spirit (the
Goddess) will express itself in the New Age Kingdom to
come as a political entity to become known as *World
Governmental Control Group*. This elite group will consist
of a small core of men and women who will literally reign
as kings or presidents over the whole earth. They will,
Alder explains, work together and give their strength and
power to the New Age Christ.[8]

Could this be the same group of world leaders mentioned in Revelation 17--the ten later day rulers or kings--
the ten horns of the beast--who will give their strength
and power unto the beast so that the last days Kingdom of
evil will be formed on planet earth?

The Spirit of Oneness

For his own purposes, Satan has inspired his New Age occultists to create the fiction of the Goddess and to put forth a doctrine and theology that the Goddess is the Holy Spirit of God. As Kim Miller, a Christian leader who has studied the New Age in much depth, discloses, "the counterfeit of the Holy Spirit in New Age theology is the concept of energy. . . . The energy is characterized as feminine in form."[9]

Now, it should be understood that although the New Age and the occult worship each of the three deities of the unholy trinity, including the Goddess and the son to come, Satan makes clear that ultimately it is *he alone* who will be worshipped. This worship of Satan alone as the supreme deity is guaranteed by the New Age teaching of *Oneness.*

The oneness doctrine of the New Age suggests that the Mystery Woman (Spirit) and the Father of Light (Satan) are One. They are an androgynous duo, a combination of the male and feminine principles. As Eckankar founder Paul Twitchell explains in *The Flute of God*, "For this reason we have been told that the Oneness of Spirit is the foundation of all commandments.[10] Twitchell goes on to state that the creation of the universe came then from a single power. He further explains that the mystery religion understands that "Instead of a twin power there was (and is) only the singular power which looked like a masculine power only:"

> If it is possible to put the cosmic principle into words, it is
> that God is One, and that this 'one' finds a center in
> ourselves, which means the result will center in ourselves,
> which in turn means the result will be new creation in and
> from ourselves. We shall realize in ourselves the working

of a principle whose distinguished feature is its simplicity.
It is oneness . . . Unity.[11]

This teaching is highly significant. Of course we see
that the New Age continues its unholy counterfeiting, for
we know that the Bible teaches that the Lord our God is
One God and that while we worship God as Father, Son
and Holy Spirit, these Three are at the same time One.
Now comes Satan's New Age with the ultimate forgery
and false claim, that the Father of Light and the Goddess,
the androgynous pair, are One, and that in time they will
be joined by their Son to constitute an Unholy Trinity.
Yet, this unholy trinity is seen ultimately as "a masculine
power only."[12]   Satan does not plan to share his throne
with anyone--no, not even with a fictitious mistress.

The New Age teaching is that by "centering," a
principle and technique often employing visualization and
meditation techniques by which the person focuses all his
or her mental energies on a spiritual object or goal,
women and men can become one with "God." This is the
principle of *holism*, the holistic person. It is also what the
oriental concept of yin/yang involves. Again, we also can
return to the psychological concepts of *psychosynthesis*,
integration, and *individuation*, all of which refer to our
coming into a holistic, unitary relationship with an evil
power, that is, Satan.

Now we can understand why Satan is frantically
pushing the Unity Movement. As a stepping stone to him,
he currently allows his followers to worship him under
many different names. He has even created a fictional
Goddess who many adore and venerate. But ultimately,
Satan will demand that all of mankind *worship him alone*.
Even the lie of the Goddess will come to an end. In his
insane jealousy, Satan, incarnated into the Antichrist, will
one day mandate that every person who does not worship
him *directly* will be put to death.

Images of the Goddess from currently popular goddess/New Age magazines and tabloids.

An image will be erected. All must pay homage to this image and receive the mark of the beast, either on their forehead or their right hand. How do we know this? Simply because it is recorded in Revelation 13 of our Bible. Every prophecy that was ever given in our Bible came to pass, and this too will transpire.

Satan Invites You to Become One With Him

As Paul Twitchell explained, the New Age goal is for individuals to center themselves with and in the One, who in reality is Satan. To that end, the New Age promotes such centering techniques as meditation, centering prayers, and centering through visualization. Through such centering, it is taught, oneness can be achieved. All this really means is that you can be one with the Goddess and with the Force that lies behind her myth. The New Age likes to call this "linking up with the universe" or "experiencing the connectedness of all things." Christians call it what it is: *possession.*

When a woman takes on the characteristics of the Goddess, the Goddess will incarnate in her. As the incarnation of the Goddess, she then can also experience the oneness with the supreme being. This was and is the final goal and objective of the Mystery Babylon religions:

> The final goal, the final objective of all the *Mysteries,* was the full realization by the initiate of his divine nature in its oneness with the Supreme Being--by whatever name called--who is the Universe in all its phases and in its wholeness and completeness.[13]

The Goddess is a Mythical Fiction of Satan

Let us then cut through all of the nonsense and the mysterious phraseology of the New Age and its teachings on the Goddess and her Master and simply state the obvious, unvarnished Truth as revealed in our Bible. The Goddess is a myth, a fictitious creation of Satan. In reality she represents the Whore of Babylon, the woman with the cup full of filthiness and the abomination of her fornications. The Goddess simply is the unholy spirit that snakes its way in and out, through and through, pervading every aspect of the New Age World Religion. The Goddess is the Unholy Spirit of Satan. And since *he* is the serpent, so is she also, for she is the mirror image of him.

The Corruption of the Serpent

The serpent beguiled Eve in the garden. Today he seeks to beguile, to entrance, enchant, and charm you and I. His New Age wishes to corrupt our bodies and minds from the simplicity that is in Christ Jesus.

> But I fear, lest by any means, as the serpent beguiled Eve through his subtly, so your minds should be corrupted from the simplicity that is in Christ.

> For if he that cometh preacheth another Jesus, whom we have not preached, *or if ye receive another spirit,* which you have not received, or another gospel, which you have not accepted, ye might well bear with him (II Corinthians 11:3).

There are today many false "Jesuses" running to and fro, sponsored by various New Age churches, cults, and groups. And there is "another gospel" of the New Age. Where did these abominations first originate? The answer can only be: *Babylon.*

SIX

Sins of Mystery Babylon

Therefore, behold, the days come, that I will do judgement upon the graven images of Babylon. . . . As Babylon hath caused the slain of Israel to fall, so at Babylon shall fall all the slain of the earth.
(Jeremiah 51:47, 49)

The (New Age) spiritual path seems to have a special connection to the Story of Babel since the builders of Shinar sought to build a tower to reach to the heavens. . . . We, too, are reaching to the heavens . . . like the builders of the Biblical tower in Babylon.
Magical Blend magazine
(Issue 15, 1987)

One of the most hideous and revolting images in the Bible is the description in Revelation of the great whore that sits upon many waters. Astride a scarlet-colored beast, full of names of blasphemy and having seven heads and ten horns, the woman:

was arrayed in purple and scarlet color, and decked with gold and precious stones and pearls, having a golden cup in

her hand full of abominations and filthiness of her
fornication.

And upon her forehead was a name written, MYSTERY,
BABYLON THE GREAT, THE MOTHER OF
HARLOTS AND ABOMINATIONS OF THE EARTH
(Revelation 17:4-5).

John also tells us that he saw this scarlet woman
drunken with the blood of the saints and with the blood of
the martyrs of Jesus: "And when I saw her I wondered
with great admiration."

The angel who carried John in the spirit into the
wilderness and showed him this vision made clear to him
that this repugnant and bloody harlot symbolized the dark,
satanic religious system that would, in the last days, grow
in power and strength until it encompassed the earth.
This end-time Church of Satan, The Whore of Babylon, is
to have dominion over "peoples, multitudes, nations, and
tongues." Hers is a unity-conscious, one world religion
that will give its wicked spirituality over to the Antichrist.

Several years ago when I first began to research the
New Age Movement, I had no idea at all that this fast
growth religious malignancy was related to the vision
about the woman on the scarlet-colored beast described
so vividly in Revelation. However, Texe and I had begun
to encounter a number of friends in scientific and
technological circles who had told us of the new "scientific
spirituality" they were experiencing. I was shocked to
discover that some of our friends were actually practicing
psychic surgery and channeling dead spirits from beyond.
A few were involved in still darker sorcery and occult
pursuits. I simply could not understand how otherwise
intelligent, well-educated men and women could let
themselves be hoodwinked into believing in such patently
dangerous, pseudo-scientific, unChristian practices.

What I found out when I closely examined the mushrooming, fast-growth New Age network was truly appalling. What our friends called "The New Thought Religion" is not some small and insignificant splinter "Christian" church, nor is it simply an eccentric scientific cult, or a harmless off-beat philosophical group. *It is a massive, worldwide religious system devoid of morality* and founded on the satanic premise that man is himself an evolving God. The New Age is a world religion. Indeed, *it is the fastest growing religion on earth.*

In embracing this New Age world religion, our friends had been sucked into a godless vacuum from which few can escape. Furthermore, *none* can do so without the unequalled redemptive powers of Jesus Christ.

Like other New Agers, our friends had become convinced that traditional Christianity was a dying religion and that it needed a higher level of consciousness to revive itself. Their leaders in the New Age, also called the *Age of Aquarius,* had painted for them the bold outlines of a totally new, unified one world religion in which men of all races, colors, and creeds live in peace and harmony as brothers, sharing and loving. This new world religion, they were led to believe, would guarantee the end of world hunger, war and discord.

This propaganda, of course, is all part of the Lie, but it is effective in attracting converts to the New Age. A major part of this Lie is the satanic myth that a New Age "Christ"--not Jesus!--is coming soon to seize the reigns of world power, unify all religions, and inspire men to godhood. Our friends especially liked the New Age doctrine that they were already gods and had a goddess or god within; they simply needed to "awaken" to their divinity.

After reviewing thousands of articles, speeches, books and other paraphernalia and literature of the New Age movement, and learning close-up of its doctrines and objectives, both Texe and I found our spirits deeply grieved. Here was the worldwide religious system envisioned by John and recorded in Revelation, chapter 17. Here was the beast and its deadly, blasphemous end-time church; here was the revival of MYSTERY, BABYLON THE GREAT, THE MOTHER OF HARLOTS AND ABOMINATIONS OF THE EARTH. Prophecy was being revealed before our very eyes.

We determined that if we were to fully understand the deep significance and meaning of this modern-day Baal religion--if we wanted to help our friends as well as many others escape the great Lie of the New Age, we would have to travel back to the beginnings. It would be necessary to discover the roots of this occult system. After all, today's New Age is simply a revival of ancient Babylon, a reawakening of the religion that Abraham confronted, that Moses fought spiritual warfare against, and that the Apostle Paul exposed in Ephesus, Corinth, Athens and elsewhere.

Even a cursory look at the idolatrous religious system of the early Babylonian Empire should convince the most hardened skeptic that this wicked and polluted system has once again risen its beastly head in the form of the New Age World Religion.

Just what was the religion of ancient Babylon? How did it begin? And why does the Bible prophesy the revival of Babylon in the last days?

The Rise of Babylon, That Great City of Wickedness

Babylon was one of the greatest cities of the ancient world. It was founded by Nimrod, described in the Bible as a "mighty hunter before the Lord" (Genesis 10:8-9). Nimrod, aided by his adulterous but beautiful wife, Semiramis, sought to build the Tower of Babel. However,

God confounded their evil intentions by causing the builders to speak in a variety of confusing languages.[1]

The New Age seeks today to "rebuild" the Tower of Babel and re-create the one world order of Mystery Babylon.

As King, Nimrod was a superb warrior and conqueror, expanding Babylon's boundaries throughout Sumeria and Mesopotamia. Eventually, the lands of Egypt and India also came under the cultural, economic, and military domination of Babylon.

Babylon was to become a fantastic city with wide avenues, large buildings, and tall towers. Its famous hanging gardens were reputed to be one of the seven wonders of the world. Huge libraries were built, stocked with scientific and other kinds of books and tablets. By the time the glory of Babylon had finally faded, centuries after Nimrod, the wealth and beauty of this great city and its far-flung empire surpassed all others. Werner Keller, noted Bible historian, has written:

> Babylon, as an international centre of trade, industry, and commerce was the great school for the cities and capitals of the whole world. . . . The metropolis, whose ruins after 2,500 years still betray its ancient power and glory, had no equal in the ancient world.[2]

Nimrod, being the founder of this great empire, was soon the object of worship by his subjects. The people had begun to deify Nimrod when, suddenly, he died. History is hazy on the cause of his death, but apparently he was defeated in battle and his body cut up into pieces and distributed throughout the empire.

The Mother Goddess and Her Satanic Religion

Semiramis, Nimrod's queen, was clever and diabolical. She spread far and wide the doctrine that Nimrod had not died. He had merely gone on to a heavenly abode where he sat as God of Gods and Master of All--a man-deity worthy of mankind's devotion and worship. Semiramis' son, who later became her incestual husband, was claimed to be the Son of God. This naturally made Semiramis herself the "Mother of God." This was the Satanic Trinity: Father, Mother, Son--the prime gods and goddess of a perverse universe.

Semiramis developed a counterfeit religious system based on this unholy trinity which was laced with idolatry, sensuality, black magic arts, and the occult. She was reputed to be the most lovely woman on earth and soon this religion focused on her supposed spiritual greatness, her supernatural powers, and her voluptuous physical beauty.[3]

Semiramis, the Mother Goddess, was also called the Queen of Heaven. She bedecked herself with jewels and gold and spread the doctrine that those who followed her and were initiated into the "Mysteries" would be prosperous, gain abundant material wealth, and enjoy sexual ecstasy as spiritual gifts from the gods. Drunkenness and merriment was a prime feature of worship as revelers lifted their cups and chanted praises to the goddess. Sexual orgies then followed a revealing of the Mysteries, the secretive, satanic doctrines that were taught by Babylonian priests and priestesses.

Today, the sexual rituals and licentiousness of Babylon are back, introduced into modern-day society by the New Age.

The Babylonian Mystery Religion was so carnally seductive that it appealed mightily to the lustful natures of men and women everywhere. As a result, the religion was quickly hailed and accepted throughout all the nations and peoples of the world. The goddess Semiramis, her husband and son, began to be worshipped under other names by people of other cultures and nations. In India, Semiramis was called Mother Kali, Brahmin was the father figure, and Shiva or Krishna the son. In Egypt, the Mystery Religion worshipped Isis as Mother Goddess, Osiris as the Father God, and Horus as the Son God. You'll recall that in the desert, the people of Israel, during the absence of Moses, began anew the worship of the golden calf, the image of this Egyptian trinity of deities.

Later, in Greece, the fame of the Mother Goddess and her Mystery cults spread into Phoenicia and all of Asia Minor. The Babylonian religion also found favor in Rome, Germany, Spain, and Britain. Diana of the

I, ISIS AM ALL THAT HAS BEEN, THAT IS OR SHALL BE; NO MORTAL MAN HATH EVER ME UNVEILED.

THE FRUIT WHICH I HAVE BROUGHT FORTH IS THE "SUN"

An artist's depiction of Isis, the sensuous Mother Goddess worshipped in Egypt. Isis wore a thin scarlet (red) colored veil on her body, just as does the Whore of Babylon (see Revelation 13).

Ephesians was an incarnation of the Mother Goddess, as was Venus, the Roman goddess of love and beauty, and Aphrodite, the Greek goddess of sex and love. Most popular in Rome was the goddess Cybele and her son Fortuna. It was thought that Cybele gave Rome its magnificent military victory over Hannibal and his invading elephants. This belief spurred Roman devotion to the goddess mystery cults.

In Babylon itself, the names Ishtar, Astarte, and Beltis were the most popular forms of addressing the Mother Goddess. The name Nimrod gave way to worship of the same god by the names of Ashteroth, or Belus (shortened to Bel or Baal, so often mentioned in the Bible).

There were also many other names attributed to the goddess of Babylon. So many that she came to be known as the "Goddess with 10,000 faces."

Three-in-One: The Unholy Babylonian Trinity

As we have seen, the Babylonians believed in an unholy Triune God made up of the Father, the Mother, and the Son--clearly a deliberate mocking and perversion by Satan of the Holy Trinity of God, His Son, and the Holy Spirit. In worshipping either the feminine goddess or the masculine god, it was thought that the other was also being venerated.

Babylon had become the source from which all systems of idolatry flowed. Wherever the Mother Goddess Mystery Religion flourished, idols were cast from bronze, gold, or other metals, and hewn from wood and stone. Alexander Hislop, in his remarkable 19th century work, *The Two Babylons*, documented how the Mystery Religion of Babylon assimilated all the other pagan religions throughout the nations. It was also the principal spiritual enemy of the early Christian church of the Book of Acts.[4]

This idolatrous religious system also showed up periodically among the Jews. God's wrath was repeatedly kindled at the apostate leaders of His chosen people who led their people into worship of Tammuz, Baal, Ashteroth, and Asherah, the Mother Goddess (called the "Queen of Heaven" by heretical Jews).

Exclaimed Isaiah, "How is the faithful city become a harlot!" (Isaiah 1:21) Also see Jeremiah 10:1-14; 44:3; 44:15-25; Judges 10; Exodus 32:6; II Kings 23:11.

It was because of their abominations in despoiling the temple by erecting images of the Queen of Heaven and by sacrificing their children to the fire gods of Babylon that God set about to punish the defiant Jews for their iniquity. First, in the 6th century BC, He brought them into captivity in Babylon. Then in 70 AD, Jerusalem was sacked and burned by the Roman General Titus.[5] The Jewish people were dispersed. Israel was extinguished as an independent Hebrew nation until almost 1900 years later when, in 1948, God miraculously restored the Jewish people to their ancient homelands in Palestine.

Babylon: The Wounded Beast

Babylon, one of the world's mightiest empires, fell to Persian conqueror Cyrus the Great, "God's Anointed" (see Isaiah 45:1), in 539 BC. Its fall had been prophesied by Jeremiah, Isaiah and other Old Testament prophets. Jeremiah announced:

> Babylon hath been a golden cup in the Lord's hand, that made all the earth drunken: the nations have drunk of her wine; therefore the nations are mad (Jeremiah 51:7).

Bearing in mind the Mystery of Iniquity that was Babylon the Great, Isaiah declared this judgment of the Lord:

> And Babylon, the glory of kingdoms, the beauty of the Chaldees excellency, shall be as when God overthrew Sodom and Gomorrah. It shall never be inhabited, neither shall it be dwelt in from generation unto generation (Isaiah 13:19-20).

God's prophecies are never off the mark and so Babylon fell to its dreaded enemy Cyrus the Great. Later, the Persian ruler Xerxes destroyed part of the city to punish the people for continued rebellion. Subsequently, the city was totally pillaged and became ruins. Once the fount of every perverse and wicked practice on earth, Babylon as a great city and empire was never again to be heard from.

The power of Bible prophecy, however, was proven when the apostle John, long after Babylon was destroyed as a world military, commercial, and political power, wrote in Revelation 17 of "Mystery Babylon, Mother of Harlots." John's inspired writings clearly describe a latter days, rejuvenated and renewed Babylonian religious and government system having global dominion.

This seeming discrepancy is easily explained when we realize that, while Babylon *the city* had been erased from the world's register of powerful empires, the horrendous *Mystery Religious System* of Babylon continued to live on in other nations throughout the known world! Babylon's religious poison had traveled and been ingested by people and nations in India, Tibet, China, Egypt, Greece, Rome and elsewhere.

The angel who brought to John his vision of Revelation called Babylon "the beast that was, and is not, and yet is" (Revelation 17:8). Also observe that

Revelation speaks of the fall of *two Babylons*. In Revelation 13:1-5, prophecy reveals that the Beast that is Babylon is first "wounded to death," but then "his deadly wound was healed: and all the world wondered after the beast."

Babylon Lives!

After the fall of Babylon, its priests and priestesses moved the headquarters of their foul mystery religious system to Pergamos in Asia Minor, which was identified in the Bible as "where Satan's seat is" (Revelation 3:13). From its cult center in Pergamos, the malicious doctrines of Satan's Babylon flowed to Rome and far, far beyond. Babylon lived on, being fed by demonic spirits from below.

Much mention is made in the New Testament of the Mystery cults which Paul and the early Christians encountered in the early years after the death, resurrection and ascension of Jesus. In Ephesus, Paul was forced to depart when silversmiths riled an angry mob against the apostle, making it impossible for him to preach above the din and roar of the crowd. The craftsmen were alarmed because they were afraid the new Christian faith taught by Paul would take away the profits they derived from creating souvenir idols of their goddess, Diana, "whom Asia and all the earth worshipped" (Acts 19:27). Diana was simply another incarnation of the Babylonian Mother Goddess. Today, Diana is the preferred Goddess of witchcraft covens.

In the capitol city of Rome, reprobate followers of the Mystery Religion and its many cults incited the populace against the Christians. Thus began the tremendous persecution of Christians by the Emperor Nero and his successors, who viewed Jesus Christ and his growing band of supporters a threat to a Roman Empire rooted in such

Babylonian sins as sexual decadence, economic plunder, and military conquest.

The Goddess is shown here as an amazon-like warrior. Note the occultic symbols and "power" animals shown on her body suit. The three spears represent the unholy trinity.

Christianity prevailed, however, because it was God's will that Jesus be taught to the whole world. Beginning in the year 312 A.D., after the Roman Emperor Constantine converted to the Christian faith, the Mystery religions and cults throughout the empire that once were so powerful and mighty began to be suppressed by the authorities. To survive, they were forced to go underground, where they have continued over the centuries as hidden religious orders and secretive witch's covens.

In addition, the organized Catholic Church, which unified and succeeded the early independent Christian congregations, integrated into its body of doctrine and in its sacraments and rituals some of the most notorious practices and doctrines of the outlawed Babylonian mystery religion and cults. Among those adopted: the worship of idols, the exchange of money for religious favors, the practice of confessing one's sins to a priest, and the false doctrine that Mary is Eternal Virgin, Co-redeemer, Confessor, Mediatrix, Queen of Heaven and Mother of God. Mary thus became, for many, the Mother Goddess, a practice that continues to this day.

What we realize when we trace the history of Babylon's wicked religion is that the Beast that is the church of Satan has not yet been finally overcome. The second and final fall of Babylon has yet to come, awaiting the return to earth of Jesus Christ. Mystery Babylon lived on, and today, Satan has a Plan to resurrect his great, idolatrous religious system and bring it to even more glorious heights than it ever enjoyed in its majestic days in ancient Babylon. This Plan, already being worked-- successfully thus far--is to unify all the religions and governments of the world into one, combined system under the mantle of the New Age.

Babylon, Yesterday and Today

If the New Age World Religion is the modern-day revival of the mystery religion of ancient Babylon and Rome, there should be direct, undeniable parallels between the two systems. Do such parallels exist? Can they be documented?

Our research into the doctrine and ritual of the Babylonian Mystery and New Age world religions has uncovered many striking parallels. These remarkable sim- ilarities provide definitive, unerring proof that the two anti-Christian religious systems are, in fact, one and the same.

The practices, rituals, and doctrines common to both the Mystery Religion and cults of Babylon and to the New Age World Religion include all of the following:

Drug/alcohol abuse Numerology
Palmistry Shamanism
Sacred music Animism
Chants Incense
Fire worship Herbology
Gemology Demonic healing
Visualization Psychic/Mind powers
Meditation Magical words
Astral travel Goddess worship
Hypnotism Witchcraft
Levitation Sexual licentiousness
Astrology Occult symbolism
Reincarnation Idolatry
Evolution Karma
Divination Self-love
Man-god doctrine Infanticide/abortion
Nature worship (sun, moon, earth, etc.)
Prosperity from gods doctrine
Polytheism (multiple gods)
Personal transformation (rebirth)
Merging of science, religion, and government
Spiritism/spiritualism
Necromancy (communication with the dead)
Sex magic (or magick)
Oracular magic
Mystery teachings and initiation
Altered states of consciousness

It is important that we realize who is the originator of these ungodly doctrines, rituals and practices. The one responsible is the real god of the New Age. His name is Lucifer.

Is Lucifer Man's Benefactor?

The *Gnostic* sects of the second and third centuries, whose doctrines were patterned after those of Babylon's Mystery cults, taught that Lucifer was man's benefactor. It was he, they thought, who, in the Garden of Eden, persuaded Eve to eat of the forbidden fruit, thereby giving man the gift of knowledge of good and evil.

These sects also taught that after a struggle in the heavens, the "true god" (Lucifer) was unfairly banished to the "lower world." According to this heretical gnostic teaching, at the end of time the true god will ascend to the "upper world," defeat the false God who dethroned him, and regain his rightful place as Master of the Universe and God of gods.

These same false teachings are today being promoted by the New Age, whose leaders seek to rehabilitate Lucifer as man's benefactor and lord. Matthew Fox, a Catholic priest who is also an ardent New Ager, has even written a book which reinterprets the account in Genesis of Adam and Eve. Its title is *Original Blessing,* a mockery of the term "original sin." Like other top New Age "theologians," Fox teaches that Eve and Satan did man a favor and service in the garden. It was their act, he writes, that established men and women on the path toward full divinity.[6] The New Age further teaches that the knowledge (gnosis) gained first by Eve, then by Adam, was essential as a cardinal step toward godhood for all humanity. Eve thus becomes the model for today's woman who desires to be all she can become.

New Age Mystery Teachings and Initiation

The cults of Babylon and its imitators in Rome, Egypt and elsewhere were *Mystery* religions.   Believers celebrated secret and sacred rites into which they were *initiated*. Only through initiation could an individual expect to acquire the deep wisdom and knowledge and the promise of immortality that the god offered.

Many New Age cults and groups require similar initiation stages. They pride themselves on being Mystery religions and they boastfully brag to recruits that they have hidden Mysteries and secrets to offer--after the proper initiation.

David Spangler frankly calls the required mystical initiation of the New Age the "Luciferic Initiation," describing it as "the particular doorway through which the individual must pass if he is to come fully into the presence of his (Lucifer's) light and his wholeness."[7]

In Babylon, men were told that initiation into the Mysteries was an essential step toward achieving man-god status. This, too, is the New Age's radiant promise to the initiate.   But initiation comes with a high price: the newcomer must prove he is a loyal disciple and a dedicated believer in New Age religious dogma.   As Lola Davis explains:

> We recognize, as did the Mystery schools, that spiritual knowledge is so powerful that it can be entrusted only to those who will use it for the good of humanity. For this reason, spiritual laws will be taught in states and only after students demonstrate the ability to use their knowledge for the good of mankind.[8]

Though the New Age shrouds its teachings in mystery and claims that its initiates seek only "the good of mankind," we can sum up these hidden secrets in one word: *Satanism*. Gradually and in stages, the initiate learns to trust in Satan as his master and comes to believe in Satan's great Lie that man is god and Lucifer is the Way and is the Father of Light. This is the mystery available *only to the initiate*.

In contrast, the message of salvation in our Bible is open to all. Jesus told us not to fear those who practice the Mystery religions: "Fear them not therefore: for there is nothing covered, that shall not be revealed; and hid, that shall not be known" (Matthew 10:26-27). The Apostle Paul professed that he was called as a minister so that the word of God may be fully revealed:

> Even the mystery which hath been hid from ages and from generations, *but now is made manifest to his saints*: to whom God would make known what is the riches of the glory of this mystery among the Gentiles; which is Christ in you, the hope of glory . . . that we may present every man perfect in Christ Jesus (Colossians 1:26-28).

The most wonderful secret of all time can now be told! The Mystery of the Ages has been fully revealed in our Bible; the Good News has been published and proclaimed: Jesus is Lord.

Beyond God the Father: New Age Goddess Worship

We have seen how Satan's Babylonian Mystery Religion exalted the Mother Goddess and held her up as the supreme god of the universe. Likewise, many in today's New Age World Religion point to the supremacy of the goddess. Some believe that their coming New Age Messiah, or "Christ," will be a woman. Most, however, believe that while their New Age "Christ" will come as a man, that man will be a reincarnation of the triune god of the Babylonians: a trinity that has as its head the figure of the Mother Goddess.

The New Age Plan, therefore, is to implant into the minds of all humanity that the Mother Goddess is alive, and that she alone is to be worshipped and adored. The strategy is to feminize all religions, including Christianity.

There can be little doubt that this ingenious strategy of the evil one has proven effective. Its effectiveness has already been demonstrated in a number of cases. Mary Baker Eddy, founder of the Christian Scientists and a forerunner of today's New Age leaders, was one of the first to assert that in the second coming the messiah would be female. Mother Ann Lee, who began the Shakers, also believed in a coming female Christ.[9]

Mocking the Bible teaching of the second coming of Jesus, feminist Rita M. Gross recently called for "the Second Coming of the Goddess." Suggesting that the goddesses of Hinduism "present one of the richest set of images," Gross remarked that we could profitably use the Hindu female deities "as a resource for the contemporary rediscovery of the Goddess." Gross also believes we can be "enriched by meditating on the Goddess."[10]

In *Beyond God the Father*, noted feminist theologian Mary Daly argues that sexist language and symbolism are essential to the core of Judaism and Christianity and that women should therefore abandon those religions. She also proposed that God be named "verb" to point to the dynamism of "Be-ing," a reference to the New Age belief that man is ever evolving into a higher consciousness and is becoming deity.[11]

Merlin Stone, in *When God Was a Woman*, says that "learning that God is a woman can help women to view themselves as being in the image and likeness of the Goddess, as creators of their own destinies and responsible for their own lives."[12] This, too, is a major New Age goal: to mold and recreate today's women into the wicked image of the goddess.

LaVedi Lafferty and Bud Hollowell, founders of the Collegians International (New Age) Church, attempt to explain the feminine aspect of the coming New Age "Christ" by referring to the androgynous (unisex) nature of reincarnated spirits. They even blasphemously point to Jesus Christ as a unisex example:

> As to the controversial immaculate conception, Jesus and Mary are considered to have been twin souls, or the male and female aspects reunified in Mary. Normally an enlightened entity reunites with the twin aspect, not as two people, but as one in one body, which may appear as either sex. [13]

Will the New Age "Christ", 666, be Bisexual?

Why is the New Age speaking of the return of the Mother Goddess when Revelation 13:18 clearly prophesies that the Beast with the number 666, the Antichrist, *will be a man*? The Babylonians taught a "oneness" doctrine, claiming that the Mother Goddess was of bisexual spirit, *being both male and female*.

The yin/yang symbol of the orient (and the New Age) represents the combining of opposites--black and white, good and evil, male and female, Satan and God--into one whole.

Now today, we see a related doctrinal concept put forth by the New Age suggesting that even though the Christ shall be a man he will possess a dual masculine/feminine spirit. He will be bisexual and androgynous. The New Age calls this either integration, psychosynthesis, individuation, or holism. This is the *yin/yang* concept, the blending of the sexes into one. It is through this process, the New Age teaches, that New Age woman and man shall themselves become gods.

The New Age is also for this same reason promoting the psychological concept of *Left Brain/Right Brain*. Though scientific research affirms that we do have left and right brain hemispheres, there is no scientific evidence whatsoever that one or the other of these hemispheres is "feminine" and creative while the other is "masculine" and logical.[14] This is a fiction created by the New Age to convince people that to be "whole," they must integrate their masculine and feminine "selves" or "poles". The androgynous bisexual is Satan's model human for the New Age.

The Antichrist to be a Man with the Goddess Within

We can therefore expect the coming Antichrist, the New Age Messiah, to be exalted by the New Age World Religion as possessing an androgynous spirit. He will be considered as a man who has perfected himself spiritually by combining his masculine and feminine "selves" into a unified whole. He will be acclaimed to be a man who has the Goddess within, a perfect embodiment of the unholy trinity.

This is why the Bible warns us about the Beast to come. It reveals that the same grotesque spirit of evil that possessed Nimrod, Semiramis, and Nero will envelop the soul of this last days "god-man." Moreover, the World Religion over which he presides will restore the same bloody acts that prevailed in Egypt and Rome. The Sins of Mystery Babylon will once again haunt the modern world.

> Christianity came face to face with the Babylonian paganism in its various forms that had been established in the Roman Empire. . .much persecution resulted. Many Christians were falsely accused, thrown to the lions, burned at the stake, and in other ways tortured and martyred. . .Over the centuries God has called his people out of the bondage of Babylon. Still today His voice is saying, "Come out of her my people, that ye be not partakers of her sins!"[15]

SEVEN

The Goddess is Back! She Lives!

*Babylon hath been a golden cup in the Lord's hand,
that made all the nations drunken: the nations have
drunk of her wine; therefore the nations are mad.*
(Jeremiah 51:7)

*The Goddess has only one commandment . . . love
life. . . . Women are designed by the cosmos to lead the
human world back, now, to the great celebration . . .
we will return to the Goddess, the Great Mother of All
Life, as her magic children . . .*
Monica Sjoo and Barbara Mor
The Great Cosmic Mother

She's back. A Mother Goddess. Satan's Mistress. Yes, the Whore of Babylon, the Mystery Woman is back. Her wound has been healed and she's come.

One of the most incredible things about the New Age World Religion is that it is an occult religion which is formed by Satan as a women's spirituality movement. In effect, the New Age is WomanChurch. Bible prophecy told us very clearly and powerfully that the last days, world-wide Church of Satan is to be represented as a woman: Mystery, Babylon the Great, the Mother of Harlots and Abominations of the Earth.

It should grieve every woman and especially every Christian woman that this is so. It should especially dismay us to realize that the woman described as Mystery, Babylon the Great, the Mother of Harlots is a woman of great beauty and feminine charm. She is, the Bible tells us, *arrayed* in purple and scarlet color and decked with precious stones and pearls, having a golden cup in her hand. The Mystery Woman of Sin does not appear to be horrid and unattractive. Quite the contrary. She is a powerful, sophisticated and sensuous female--stylish, with it, fashionable, a role model for American women as we rush forward toward the high tech, twenty-first century.

Yet, even though the Mystery Woman is alluring and erotic and unparalleled in her femininity, hers is a beauty and an attraction based on a poignant foundation of evil. In her hand is a golden cup full of abominations and filthiness of her fornication. Worse, the Mystery Woman is drunken, but not with alcohol. No, she is intoxicated, says the Bible, with the blood of the saints and with the blood of the martyrs of Jesus.

Nevertheless, so magnificent, so fantastically charming and provocative is the New Age Mystery Woman that even the apostle John exclaimed, "When I saw her I wondered with great admiration."

The New Age is Babylon Restored

What Revelation 17 discloses to us is this: That the last days religious system of the Adversary will be a restoration, a revival, a renewal of the most insidious, most diabolical, most wicked religion that ever has existed on the face of the planet earth. Babylon, asleep and wounded, shall come alive!

When we look with soberness and discernment at the New Age we have to admit the horrible truth. This is no doubt the Mystery Babylon of the Bible. The Goddess does indeed live. She's back.

As this advertisement for a doll, "Galadriel," shows, the Goddess is back. She's pictured as beautiful, golden, pure, and princess-like. This Goddess look-alike doll is created to represent a character from one of J. R. R. Tolkien's fantasy occult novels, **Lord of the Rings.**

The Whore of Babylon returns resplendent in all her seductiveness and feminine wiles. She seeks the body, the sexual energies and passion of every man. But she does not start with men. *Her first objective is to seduce the minds of women.* To this end the Mystery Woman has developed an incredible, mind-boggling strategy. Her mission is simply this: To persuade you and every other woman to be exactly like her. "I am a mysterious woman," she declares:

> All men desire me. I am mother. My will governs. All men worship me. They idolize my beauty, my charm, my intellect, my wit, my humanity, my sexual favors. I Am. And you--you can be like me. You can have a goddess within you. I can be you and you can be me. Together you and I shall be all in all--seductive, desirable, overpowering, wanted by all men, loved, cherished. With me all of your fantasies and dreams will come true. Without me, O woman, you are nothing.

New Age Leaders Declare: The Goddess is Back

"There are individuals living upon this earth," writes Paul Twitchell, founder of the New Age group Eckankar, "who are centuries old. There is said to be one, a woman, who is supposedly a million years old. Her purpose for living is destruction, and for that reason she passes from one nation to another creating havoc wherever she goes. She is known by many names. In India they call her Kali, the Mother Goddess, the goddess of destruction."[1]

Paul Twitchell is only one of scores of New Age leaders, teachers, theologians, and authorities who affirm that Mystery Babylon has returned. The Goddess is back in all her glory and with all her unparalleled magnetism and glamour. Moreover, the principal thrust of the Goddess today is to win the allegiance of every living woman. Thus, you, too, are her target. Through human agents--the leaders of today's Satanic New Age religion-- the great Cosmic Mother as she has been called, the harlot of Mystery Babylon, wants you to believe that through her you can live a life of joy, serenity, prosperity, and sexual, carnal, worldly pleasure. She offers you and every woman a sensual heaven on earth, a celebration of flesh and spirit.

Monica Sjoo and Barbara Mor, in their weighty book (over 500 pages), *The Great Cosmic Mother*, explain why, in the New Age occult view, the Goddess has returned. "If we do not want to die," they insist, "then we must evolve--and that means we must dance, expand. . .with the dancing cosmos. We return to the cosmos by becoming lovers of life."[2] It is the Goddess alone, they say, who can transform us into lovers of life:

> The Goddess . . . has only one commandment: love life. . . . Women are designed by the cosmos to lead the human world back, now, to the great celebration of the reconciliation of flesh and spirit. Thus, at the very edge of death we will return to the beginning. That is, at the end of the world (where we must surely be!) we will return to the Goddess, the Great Mother of All Life, as her magic children. . . . Now is the time to make again sacred our experience.[3]

Sjoo and Mor point out that the Goddess never really died, she simply has been sleeping these many centuries. Now she has awakened to reclaim this world for her own. Her power, they state, "cannot truly die since it is a real power of the real cosmos. It cannot die, it can only be forgotten--that means it can also be remembered, as the serpent can be awakened from its tranced sleep at the bottom of the spine and induced to rise, to become again the luminous flying bird . . ."[4]

The Bible points out that Satan is the serpent, the dragon. We recognize then the true meaning of what Sjoo and Mor are saying when they describe the Goddess, whom they claim has awakened: "In the final time of crisis, the Serpent Goddess shakes herself loose from her deep, exiled sleep in the earth's belly."[5]

The Goddess is Superior to God

The New Age contends that a Mother Goddess is greatly superior to the Christian concept of the Father God. They say that a goddess has many aspects which a Father God, a male figure, cannot have. For example, virginity, child bearing, mother love, sensitivity, and a myriad of feminine traits. Moreover, they point out that, unlike the God of the Bible, in looking back at all the mother goddesses of history, from Ashtar or Ishtar of Babylon to Isis in Egypt, Cybele in Rome, Demeter in Greece, and even Kuan Yin in ancient China, we find that the goddesses embodied both feminine *and* masculine characteristics. They were androgynous and bisexual, creator and destroyer, thus superior to the limited, patriarchal God of Judaism and Christianity.

The Catholic Church and the Goddess

The drive to bring in a Mother Goddess is especially strong among New Agers with a background of Roman Catholicism. For example, Leonardo Boff, a Franciscan priest, in his book *The Maternal Face of God*, strongly campaigns for a goddess figure to be accepted in the Church.[6] He notes first that the late Catholic priest, Pierre Teilhard de Chardin, often called the patron saint of the New Age, very much favored what is called the *feminine principle*. Chardin proposed that the planet earth was going into a new cycle in which the male god figure would be replaced by a feminine deity of spirit.

According to Chardin, the world would soon reach *Omega Point*, a grand era in which all women and men would become Christs. Collectively, humanity would become *the* Christ. But always Chardin professed that the feminine would reign over all. "The authentic pure feminine is par excellence, a luminous chaste energy, the vessel of the ideal, and of goodness," he wrote.

Moreover, Catholic priests Boff and Chardin affirmed that Mary, the mother of Jesus, was the perfect candidate to be this feminine goddess figure of the New Age. Said Chardin, "In her, as in Jesus, God is all in all."[7]

Pierre Teilhard de Chardin had much to say about the feminine principle. In one published letter, "The Eternal Feminine," he wrote as if the Mother Goddess was speaking directly through him:

> My charm can still draw men, but towards the light. I can still carry them with me, but into freedom. Henceforth, my name is virginity.[8]

Boff and Chardin certainly were not the first to attempt to deify Mary as a Mother Goddess. Indeed, in the preface of Boff's book, he quotes Pope John Paul I, who once stated: "God is Father, but, especially, mother."[9]

There is ample astonishing evidence that the official Vatican doctrine, as well as the beliefs of many millions of Catholics world-wide, has resulted in Mary literally becoming the Goddess. To these admirers, Mary is woman above all women and men, even a woman who has become greater in saving power than the Father God.

The Mother Goddess is Appealing to Women

New Age teachings on the Goddess are very appealing to many women because finally, after the many centuries of Christianity in which a male God has been worshipped, a female is fast becoming the chief deity of the planet.

Rosemary Ruether, a professor of theology at Garrett-Evangelical Theological Seminary in Evanston, Illinois, is one of the leaders in convincing women that a Mother Goddess is a boon to them in the Age of Aquarius. She states:

> Today, women are in the vanguard of the aborning civilization; and it is to the women that we look for salvation in the healing and restorative waters of Aquarius. It is to such a New Age that we look now with hope as the present age of masculism succeeds in destroying itself. . . . The rot of masculine materialism has indeed permeated all spheres of twentieth century life.[10]

Ruether speaks approvingly of the Great Goddess who "creates the universe, the earth, and the heavens, and finally creates the gods and mankind." Then, Ruether laments, "Suddenly all is ended, paradise is lost, a dark age overtakes the world . . . the Great Goddess is replaced by a stern and vengeful God."[11]

History records that temple prostitution, human sacrifice, infanticide, abortion and gruesome barbarism prevailed in the days when the goddesses reigned. But according to Ruether, when Christianity took over with its male God, women became degraded and exploited and civilization started on a downward path. Our only hope, she contends, is to exalt a mother goddess to restore and make things right once again.

In fact, Ruether believes this is already occurring. The ages of masculism, she says, are now drawing to a close. The dying days are lit up by a final flare of universal violence and despair such as the world has seldom before seen. Only the complete and total demolition of the social body, she believes, will cure the fatal sickness. Only the overthrow of the three thousand year old beast of masculist materialism will save the race. Woman will again predominate, says Ruether:

She who was revered and worshiped by early man because of her power to see the unseen will once again be the pivot . . . as divine woman.[12]

Man to Kneel to Woman in the New Age

Ruether and other New Age women leaders point out, however, that men, too, will be supremely happy in the coming New Age as they worship the Great Goddess. Ruether says that men will be invigorated. All of their energies will come to the fore. They will feel themselves the masters of the known world, she writes. The New Age man "will feel it their highest happiness to submit with gratitude to the beneficent power of womanly sympathy. In a word, Man will in those days kneel to Woman, and to Woman alone."[13]

"We Women are Going to Bring an End to God"

Another New Age authority, Naomi Goldenberg, who teaches religion at the University of Ottawa, in Ontario, Canada, as a "feminist theologian," heartily agrees with Ruether. In her book, *Changing of the Gods*, Goldenberg approvingly predicts the eventual overthrow of the existing forms of both Christianity and Judaism. "God is going to change," she writes, "we women are going to bring an end to God. We will be the end of Him."[14]

Goldenberg goes on to add that the Christian God just "won't fit anymore." The women's movement is destined, according to Goldenberg, to bring about religious changes on a massive scale, helping to lessen the influence on humanity of Christ and the Old Testament God.

Happily, Goldenberg writes: "It seems highly likely that the West is on the brink of developing a new mysticism." Witchcraft is recommended by Goldenberg as a "perfect substitute for Christianity."[15]

Witches are major promoters of the Goddess revival. Above is an ad for a witch's periodic newspaper (address deleted).

Helena Blavatsky, New Age Prophetess

It is understandable why women have such high and prominent leadership roles in the New Age. Helena Blavatsky is still considered a saint, indeed, an ascended master, to many in the New Age. In 1888 *The Secret*

Doctrine, her classic work on occultism and the New Age to come, was published. Later, in the 30s, 40s, and 50s Alice Bailey, founder of the Lucis Trust and a follower of Blavatsky's came to the fore. Over twenty books were dictated to Bailey through her demon spirit guide Djwahl Khul. These books have been read and treasured by literally millions of New Agers all over the globe.

The Hindus and the Mother Goddess Revival

Helena Blavatsky spent much of her life in India studying under the Hindus. Her dream was to create a new world in which a Babylonian form of Hinduism could be merged with western mysticism.

Today in India, the Mother Goddess continues to be worshipped by tens of millions. Many Americans, Englishmen, West Germans, and other westerners have traveled on pilgrimages to India where they were bathed in the doctrines of the Goddess. Many of them studied the writings and the works of a Hindu guru known as Swami Vivekananda, a speaker of notable spiritual power.

Vivekananda predicted "the resurgence of the Mother Goddess into the consciousness of the world's population." He claimed he had a vision that the ancient mother goddess had awakened once more and was sitting on her throne, rejuvenated and more glorious than ever. In his vision, said Vivekananda, the Goddess commanded him to "proclaim her to all the world with the voice of peace and benediction."[16]

Swami Vivekananda did much to popularize the Goddess among westerners. However, he is only one of many Hindu gurus who have brought the feminine goddess message to America and the West. Those New Agers whose interest did not lie in Hinduism have been more than happy to travel back in history, intellectually, and recapture the images of the great mother goddesses of Babylon, Egypt, Greece, Rome, the Celts and Druids of Great Britain, and the Oriental goddess figures.

Gaia, the Earth Goddess Returns

Gaia, the Greek Earth Goddess, has become popular in this decade as the environmental and ecology movements have taken shape. For example, at the California Institute of Integral Studies, April 6-10, 1988, a conference was held in which some of the top New Age personalities-- Merlin Stone, Catholic priest Matthew Fox, Susan Griffin, and others--celebrated Gaia as "the re-emergent earth goddess."

In *New Realities* magazine, the conference was advertised as one that would explore "the unitary vision of Gaia the goddess of the living earth, and the importance and relevance of the global ecological awareness symbolized by the whole earth as a living organism." In other words, the New Age proposes that the earth is literally a living entity. She is the Green Goddess, a fertility deity.

Discovering the Goddess

The New Age is thrilled that the Goddess has been reawakened. In the *Women's Spirituality Book*, author Diane Stein exclaims "The Goddess is alive; magick is afoot! Women everywhere are discovering the Goddess, learning who she is and all her names and faces, where she came from and what she means for them."

Stein remarks that men and women "are discovering that the Goddess is initially and specifically female, and in the process are discovering themselves."[17]

Another New Age writer, Scott Cunningham, in an endorsement of Stein's book, says that her book is an initiation process promoting "a joyous union with the Goddess." Cunningham insists that Stein's book is not anti-male at all but is "valuable reading for men as well."[18]

Cunningham is correct. Satan's intention is that the Goddess is for all. Mystery Babylon is not exclusively for women, for as we see in Revelation 13, *all the world* shall worship the beast except those whose names are written in the book of life of the lamb slain from the foundation of the world.

According to Diane Stein, "the Goddess is not an out there force among the four stars . . . but is here and now and living." The Goddess she says, is within everyone and all around us. "Thou art Goddess." Stein believes that all that is necessary is that we reclaim the Mother Goddess, that we relearn, remember, and revision her skills, knowledge, and rituals.[19] In other words, the Goddess is here and now. She is no longer sleeping or lost. She simply awaits each womans' discovery.

To discover the Goddess anew, Stein recommends that women create new forms of spiritual organizations and rituals. She especially recommends covens and circles run by women. Such groups, she says, to be composed of six women who democratically would constitute a coven of six high priestesses or six leaders. Each of these six high priestesses would become the Goddess at one point or another during a single ritual and would remain the Goddess when she goes home.[20] It's interesting to note the numerical prescription of Stein. Six women participate in ritual as six high priestesses and thus become six leaders of a New Age coven. Thus, 666.

EIGHT

And Her Son Shall Have the Number 666

And I stood upon the sands of the sea, and saw a beast rise up out of the sea . . .

(Revelation 13:1)

The Love Goddess rises from the Sea.

Miriam Starhawk
The Spiral Dance

Something gigantic is going on," writes Robert Muller, former Assistant Secretary-General of the United Nations and now head of the Peace University, a major New Age project. The New Age is dawning and it is "glorious and beautiful like Aphrodite emerging from the sea." [1]

What a revealing choice of phrases. Aphrodite is pagan Greece's version of the Babylonian Goddess. The Greeks pictured her as a lovely and rapturous woman rising out of a churning sea of chaos. It is fascinating that the Bible in Revelation 17:1 depicts the same Goddess as "the whore who sitteth upon many waters." Even more eye opening is Revelation 13:1 in which this last days Satanic religion is described as *a beast rising out of the sea*!

The Goddess, then, is the spiritual harlot whose efforts will someday succeed in lifting her "Son," the Antichrist, to the very pinnacle of world authority and blasphemy.

The Beast that Arises out of the Sea

There is no doubt that the Goddess is the spiritual mother of the Antichrist, whose number is to be 666. Barbara Walker, a noted historian and researcher, has written that "The Miraculous Number 666 was very, very holy in the Egyptian religion of the Goddess." Walker describes the Great Mother Goddess of Babylon as follows:

> Babylonian "star," the Great Goddess who appears in the Bible as Ashtoreth, Anath, Asherah . . . the Queen of Heaven. She was also the Great Whore, described in Revelation 17:5 or Babylon the Great, the Mother of Harlots. . . . Men communed with her through the sexual rites of her harlot princesses.[2]

Dianne Stein discusses the fact that the Goddess has been represented in history under many names--as Gaia, Ishtar, Ashtoreth, Demeter, etc. But by whatever name she is worshipped, Stein insists, it is important to note that the pagans believed the Goddess is at the origin of all things:

> The goddess of all things rose naked from Chaos and found nowhere to place her foot. Separating the sea from the sky, she brooded over the waters until she gave birth to life: herself.[3]

Though this statement is a lie in view of the true facts of creation provided us in the book of Genesis, it is amazingly accurate in terms of Bible prophecy. Here's how Revelation 13:1 describes the last days beast:

> *And I stood upon the sand of the sea, and saw a beast rise up out of the sea, having seven heads and ten horns, and upon his horns ten crowns, and upon his heads the name of blasphemy"* *(Revelation 13:1).*

> *And I saw one of his heads as it were wounded to death; and his deadly wound was healed: and all the world wondered after the beast (Revelation 13:3).*

The Goddess most definitely represents the beast system whose deadly wound was healed. We should also remember that in the Old Testament, Satan is depicted as *Leviathan,* a sea serpent. It is no accident then, that New Agers have called the Goddess the *Serpent Goddess.* And in many of the mythologies, the Goddess is pictured as a mermaid: half woman, half sea creature. The ancient Canaanites, for example, worshiped Dagon, the fish god. The Cretins worshiped the Snake Goddess. In Great Britain we have the legend of the Lochness Monster. And of course, the movie industry has immortalized and practically glamorized this beast who rises out of the sea in such classic horror films as *The Creature from the Black Lagoon.*

Recent movies such as *Splash* which bring us the image of the mermaid are helping to "awaken" the Goddess in women. This is no accident. As one prominent New Age writer recently noted, the ancient pagan Sea Goddess and the conventional figure of the mermaid both express the New Age concept that "The Love Goddess rises from the sea." [4]

*This "innovative" company offers occult and magical products by
mail, using a seductive Goddess figure and New Age altar as a
lure. The name of this firm, Mermade ("Mermaid"), is a
reference to the beast that rises from the sea of Revelation 13:1
(address of firm deleted).*

Snow White and Sleeping Beauty: Tales of the Goddess?

Popular mythologies also are reminiscent of the Mother
Goddess.   For example, New Age teacher Demetra
George, an astrologer and publisher who believes strongly
in the Goddess, has written that the stories of Snow White
and Sleeping Beauty are in reality tales of the Mother
Goddess coming alive, awakening, after a long sleep.
According to George, "These virgin goddesses fell into
swoons but now we feel her (the Goddess) awakening.
The Goddess who was in the dark moon phase has now
come into her power."

As Snow White and Sleeping Beauty awakened, our generation has witnessed a recent emergence of a women's movement into our world. New aspects of feminine expression are entering into the consciousness of humanity, and seed possibilities of a feminine defined creativity and intelligence are sprouting. This is evidenced in the widespread entrance of women into politics, arts, education, sports, and other professional careers. There has been a rediscovery of women's history and a revival of the Goddess in women's spirituality.

We're now witnessing the reemerging of the Goddess as she currently reenters the new moon phase of her cycle . . . feminine energy that has purified and regenerated its form. The Goddess has renewed her virginity. Like a youthful maiden she once again comes forth--vibrant and expectant, with visions for a future of open possibilities.[5]

As we shall see, Demetra is at least partially correct. The Goddess is back, and it may well be that she has "a future of open possibilities." But those possibilities will some day in the future cease to be open. God's Plan will prevail. The reign of the Goddess shall be for a very brief time only and then she too shall be destroyed by Satan. Satan is a destroyer, and even the Goddess, the myth that he created back in Babylon and has now restored to vitality, will not survive (Revelation 13:16).

But for now, this image of the Goddess, according to Bible prophecy, is destined to sweep forth onto the world scene. Just as Demetra George notes, the Goddess is back--purified, regenerated, renewed.

The New Age Exalts the Awakened Goddess

It is difficult today to examine even a single New Age book, magazine, or publication or to listen to even one speech or seminar talk by a New Age leader without recognizing the Mother Goddess doctrine being taught and discussed and presented. For example, in a recent issue of *Magical Blend* magazine, in an article discussing divination and soothsaying through the use of tarot cards, author Maude Reinertsen discusses "the Divine Mother." She waxes eloquence when she talks of the Mother. The Divine Mother is called "that Great Goddess, the empress of tarot, queen of queens and mother of mothers."[6] Reinertsen writes:

> She whose majesty inspires reverence and awe in the hearts of those who know her, she whose art all other artists imitate, she who indulges her children's every whelm, she whom we all know and love as mother nature. As Isis the universe is her throne, as Venus she is the patron of art, love and beauty. As Eve she is the pleasure in the garden of earthly delights. . . . She is the creative imagination at work.[7]

The Coming New Age World Religion of the Goddess

The New Age goal is nothing less than to establish Mystery Babylon as the sole world-wide religion. To that end the Goddess is being exalted as the prime deity which people everywhere should worship and obey. As one New Age teacher, a prominent feminist theologian, has said, "A new religion is being born." In the book, *WomenChurch* is proposed a universal prayer to the Goddess. One of the stanzas is as follows:

> Holy Maiden, inspire us now and all the days of our life, Amen. Holy Mother, inspire us now. Holy Wisdom, inspire us now.[8]

Rosemary Ruether, one of the chief advocates of this new religion, has written that it will be a "new kind of Christianity freed from the bonds of patriarchy and purified of the last vestiges of sexism, clericalism, and militarism." [9]

The Secret Power Behind the Throne of the Goddess

The New Age Goddess religion was destined to be. However, as we have discovered, there is a male figure behind this Goddess movement, a secretive entity whom Alice Bailey, Benjamin Creme and other New Agers tantalizingly refer to as "the one about whom nought may be spoken." However, we who know God's Word and read Bible prophecy well know who this secretive entity is. It is none other than Satan or Lucifer, the dragon, the serpent, the great adversary of God whose doom has already been foreordained by the Lord and recorded in advance in Bible prophecy:

> And the devil that deceived them was cast into the lake of fire and brimstone where the beast and the false prophet are, and shall be tormented day and night for ever and ever (Revelation 20:10).

The Goddess and Feminist Catholicism

The extent to which the Goddess Religion of the New Age has penetrated many Christian churches and pseudo-Christian churches is remarkable, if not astonishing. It's invasion of the liberal churches and of the Roman Catholic institution is especially notable.

To their credit, some Catholics themselves are very alarmed at the chain of events now occurring. In the conservative Catholic magazine *Fidelity* some time ago was a fascinating and revealing article, "The Goddess Goes to Washington," in which Donna Stiechen reported that in Washington, D.C., some 2500 people met for a "women in the church" conference. Most were female. Most indeed were nuns, many of whom were clad in their habits and their veils. The conference was an incredible event, a gala that affirmed the coming Goddess Religion. It appeared to be the consensus of the 2500 Catholic nuns, priests, educators, and theologians present that Christianity needs to be "corrected" by incorporating the Mother Goddess and her rituals within its institutions.[10]

One Catholic sister, Madonna Kolbenschlag, gave a blistering address to the conference. She encouraged the participants "in the name of our elder brother, Jesus" to "be a scandal" to the current system of Christianity which promotes the male God.

"The myth of the Father God," said Sister Kolbenschlag, "is largely a product of the Judeo Christian tradition. The holy one who is truth is beyond all images."[11]

According to nun Kolbenschlag, whose address was widely and enthusiastically received by the audience, the male God of Christianity is a "false God" who has "created the world we live in." It is therefore necessary, she urged, to create a "spirituality of a different kind."

We must recreate a "new myth" of God, remarked Kolbenschlag. She then called for a return to the ancient Goddess religion. What she really desired was a combining of the Goddess and the God into one.

Women, Kolbenschlag stated, "are clearly the catalyst for the formation of the new spirituality. It is women above all who are in the process of reversing Genesis, turning the myth on its head--and freeing their sexuality."

Finally, to cheers and applause she trumpeted this conclusion: "The holy one is breaking through the conscious of humanity as the Goddess." [12]

The priests who assembled at this conference commended the female speakers. Bishop Francis Murphy, Auxiliary of Baltimore, stated, "they are brilliant women." The Church, said Murphy, "has to incorporate a lot of modern insights." [13] Such men as Bishop Francis Murphy and Father David Power and the other male leaders present were not at all embarrassed with the proceedings. They did not even blink when Sister Kolbenschlag remarked, "Women have always experienced the inner connection of sexuality, affectivity, religious zeal, and the creative impulse. And so we have to ignore the Great Lie that denies this." [14]

In other words, Kolbenschlag and the other participants at the conference were claiming that the teaching of the Holy Bible regarding a male God is the Great Lie. This of course, has always been the Satanic tactic--to turn Truth on its end. Thus, Satan's lies become truth and God's Truth become lies.

Another Catholic theologian prominent in the Goddess movement is Matthew Fox. In his book, *The Coming of the Cosmic Christ*, Fox writes that the Christian church is dying. It is dying, he says, because it has rejected "the mother principle." "Though we love her (the Church) dearly," says Fox, "we should let her die." [15]

Fox envisions a new church being born today out of the rubble of the Christian churches. A church that will gloriously uplift the Mother, the Goddess, the feminine principle. "It is necessary," he writes, "that we all become our Mother's keeper. Mother Earth can be awakened," he assures us, though "Her pain is great now." [16]

The Fire God Trinity--Mother, Father, Son

In all of the Goddess religions of the past, women and men worshipped an unholy trinity of mother, father, and son. This is why in the temples of Greece, Rome, Babylon, Egypt, and among the Celts and Druidic sects of Gaul and Britain, were found idols and statues of a mother and son. These of course, are remarkably similar to the statues of Mother Mary and baby Jesus found in many Catholic churches today. Indeed, many of the statues of the Mother Goddess and son were simply converted by the early Catholic church toward the worship of the Christian church's Mary and Jesus. Many of the temples to the Greek Goddess Aphrodite and other manifestations of the pagan triple goddess also became Christian worship centers during the period after Constantine in which Christianity replaced the pagan religions of the Goddess.

Consistently in the writings of New Age leaders of today we find mention of a trinity, an unholy trinity. Foster Bailey of the Lucis Trust, in his revealing book, *Running God's Plan*, states that, "this trinity is . . . father, mother, child." [17] "The occult teaching," writes Bailey, "recognizes these three." Bailey also notes that the Secret Doctrine proclaims three unusual deities, which he lists as Divine Fires, Cosmic Fires, and Solar Fires. Bailey goes on to explain that the Mother aspect of the unholy trinity is the Goddess, whom he also calls Mother Earth.

Clearly the New Age promotes Mystery Babylon under the name of the Goddess. Spirit channelers, especially, have taken on this task of dredging up the Mother Goddess. One, Elwood Babbitt, has claimed to talk with Jesus Christ. The result is his book, *Talks With Christ and His Teachers*, which is very popular among many New Agers. Babbitt claims that on August 30, 1976, "Christ" came to him and made a proclamation as follows:

I am not the Saviour. I am not the star in the east. I am not the second coming. I am here, have always been so, in Energy. You see me not, yet you shall see me . . . I am the Force that pervades your being, I am your fullness, your expression. Yet I come not as that Saviour. For each is a Saviour within himself. Each is a God within himself.

It will not be long . . . before you shall see stars that will not only reflect the image of Full Energy, but define the very forms that it will take. . . . You will understand the beauty, the greatness of love and the eternal salvation of self. For truly the heavens shall shake in the strongest manner and Nature, the Mother God shall demand her right.[18]

We see, then, the recognition by the New Age that the Mother God, Nature, is the true deity of the New Age. Babbitt's lying spirit who masquerades as the "Christ" claims that he is not the Saviour, that there is no second coming, that God is simply an energy force. He, as Christ, is only a part of that energy force. However, this same demonic spirit wants us to recognize the Goddess as the supreme deity. The Goddess, Mother God, is the "image of Full Energy." She alone supposedly has the beauty, the greatness of love, and brings "the eternal salvation of self."

Babbitt's false Christ therefore goes on to say, "It is not the father nor I nor disciples . . . that shall strengthen you." [19] In other words, it is not God but the energy of the Mother Goddess who comes to restore wholeness to all women and men on planet earth.

C. S. Lewis and Other Metaphysical "Christians" Promote the Goddess Myth

It is clear that a number of well known Catholic and liberal protestant theologians, scholars, and educators are now promoting the Mother Goddess Religion. They are unholy allies of the New Age leadership and friends of the growing demonic forces of the New Age. The late C. S. Lewis, whose fantasy novels such as *Perelandra* promote the Mother Goddess, the Green Lady, as the embodiment of the green planet, was one such scholar. Lewis, whose metaphysical, non-fiction and esoteric fantasy books are wildly popular among New Agers, can properly be called the Chief Evangelist of the Mythologies. He insisted in his non-fiction works that the ancient gods and goddesses were actually authentic representatives of the God of the Bible and sub-species of Christ.

Once, while in Greece, as he and his wife, Joy, walked among the ruins of Apollo the Sun God, Lewis said that he felt a compulsion or urge to worship the pagan gods and pray to Apollo. Because of his belief that Jesus was foreshadowed by and was the fulfillment of the mythologies, C. S. Lewis did not view this as an unhealthy thought. Here's how he re-called this event:

> I had some ado to prevent Joy and myself from relapsing into Paganism in Attica! At Daphni it was hard not to pray to Apollo the Healer. But somehow one didn't feel it would have been very wrong--would have only been addressing Christ *sub specie Apollinis*.[20]

The Bible sees the Greek deity Apollo in a much different light. In Revelation 9:11 we find reference to *Apollyon* (*Apollo* was the name of the Greek God, *On* the name of the Babylonian equivalent, thus the combination: "Apollyon.") as the leader of demons in hell: "And they had a king over them, which is the angel of the bottomless pit, whose name in the Hebrew tongue is Abaddon but in the Greek tongue hath his name Apollyon."

Another writer of fantasy novels who has promoted the New Age movement is Madeleine L'Engle. L'Engle and C. S. Lewis have declared Christianity a "Myth." C. S. Lewis has written that "Jesus Christ is the fulfillment of myth." [21]

It is important to realize that to metaphysical writers such as Lewis and L'Engle, a myth is a form of "Truth." Their contention, therefore, is that the pagan myths of the many goddesses have some basis in spiritual truth. The only difference is that Lewis, for instance, believed that Jesus was the "myth that came true." [22]

In her poetic feminist book, *A Cry Like a Bell*, Madeleine L'Engle attempts to "re-tell the stories of the Christian myth," as she puts it. L'Engle suggests that the Virgin Mary be the focal point for ecumenical unity. Then, in her poem called *Isaac*, she attempts to nail the door shut to patriarchal Christianity:

> From now on, no fathers are to be trusted. . . . I know, I felt the knife at my throat before the angel stopped my father's hand.[23]

In other words, L'Engle is claiming that men, or worse, "fathers," are not to be trusted. It is significant, or course, that Jesus Christ is our Father in heaven. Thus, Madeleine L'Engle is making a direct attack on the fatherhood of God.

It is undoubtedly no accident that L'Engle is the librarian at St. John the Divine Cathedral. This is a New Age temple, basically, though its heretical pastor is affiliated with the Episcopal Church. St. John the Divine Cathedral has housed a statue of Buddha. Also, Jesus was taken down from the life-size crucifix behind the altar and a very shapely and comely female, "Crista" was placed thereon.[24]

Such unseemly attacks on Jesus should serve as coarse reminders that the New Age is unquestionably the religion of the serpent, and of the beast, Leviathan, that rises out of the sea.

NINE

The Goddess and the Serpent

And the Lord God said unto the serpent, Because thou hast done this thing, thou art cursed . . .
(Genesis 3:14)

I believe that it is time for us to reclaim the positive dimensions of serpent power in ourselves.
Alexandra Kovats
Creation magazine

The New Age leadership laughs and cackles, "There is no Satan, no devil, no boilingly hot place where sulphurous gases choke the nostrils and where flames leap and dance and people twist in agony." This is what they tell us. It is a convenient Lie. If there is no hell, of course, then there is no Satan who stalks the earth with his demons searching for souls to possess. And, if there is no Satan, then, of course, the Goddess is benign. Perhaps more than simply benign. She is the embodiment of universal goodness and deserves all homage and honor. After all, suggests the New Age, did not God lie to us in the Bible when He claimed that there was a hell and a Satan and a judgement? Should we not therefore trust the Goddess instead?

The New Age deception runs very deep. Yet, I am convinced that somewhere lurking in the heart and mind of almost of every New Age follower is a small spark of truth.   These men and women surely realize that something is amiss about the New Age.   Yet, in their desperation to escape guilt and judgement, and in their futile but frantic efforts to shield themselves from the recognition that they are sinful beings and need God's forgiveness, they willingly have become participants in the Great Myth created by Satan in these last days.

Paul Twitchell, the founder of Eckenkar, which has been called the "Ancient Science of Soul Travel," reflects the average thought process of the New Ager. In his book, *The Flute of God*, Twitchell at first confidently proclaims:

> We are gods of course, but gods of our own universe, and gods among other gods.   Every man, woman and child is god!   No one can dispute this basic fact of cosmic wisdom![1]

The Haunting Secret of All Secrets

Then, continuing, Twitchell suddenly shifts gears.   A piercing doubt enters into his reasoning.   "As I said before," he writes, "I am haunted--perhaps haunted by the fact that beyond my concept of God there is something else.   The secret of all secrets--and not many know what that might be.   I have had an opportunity to catch a glimpse of it, and for that very reason I feel haunted."[2]

Twitchell said no more, yet, his words should frighten the wits out of every New Ager alive today. What is "the secret of all secrets?"   What is it that Twitchell caught a glimpse of, and for that reason, is today   haunted?

Those who know Jesus Christ and have been given the gift of discernment know the answer.   Behind the fancy tinsel wrappings and the attractive glitter of the New Age is a dark and foreboding, yet hidden, reality. That reality is *Satan*. He is the creator of the New Age. It is *his* invention. In carrying out his destiny, he has put together in these last days an immense, staggering system and labyrinthe web of deception and lies so grotesque as to be undecipherable to the human mind.

The scheme of Satan is, in the New Age, called *The Plan*. Such a phrase seems to be harmless on the surface but to understand its true meaning, we must go deeper and realize just what this Plan is. Satan has long desired to transplant God. His insane goal (see Isaiah 14) is to rise higher than our Lord in the cosmos. This is what has corrupted him--this evil, carnal thought that he could be supreme in the universe. The power of God is so awesome that Satan has always been thwarted from attaining this insidious goal. Indeed, he shall always be denied this goal. After all, God is God. He is invincible. Yet, Satan has lavishly wasted the blood, toil and tears of millions of hapless human beings in his drive for world domination.

The Serpent and Dragon: Master of the New Age

It is entirely possible that most of the New Age leadership is so deluded that they do not truly realize whom it is they serve. This certainly appears to be the case. However, many apparently do understand the dark truth. Otherwise, how can we account for the following statement by Richard Roberts, a well known advocate of the New Age Goddess Religion:

> As far as I've been able to determine, every culture contains a mythology of a serpent or dragon which

represents the ancient and formidable Goddess of
nature. Being feminine . . . we may associate dragon
and serpent with the Great Mother. . . . Anyhow, the
monster . . . is symbolic of chaos.[3]

Egyptian Symbol For
Cosmic Consciousness

*The serpent has long been associated with the Goddess.
Above are depictions of the Greek Goddess Medusa, whose
hair was a nest of snakes, and the cobra, a holy Egyptian
symbol for the Goddess religion.*

Here we have a well known New Age writer, so
renowned that he traveled in ˊscholarly circles giving
seminars with Joseph Campbell, the late, famed author
of many, many books on mythologies, nonchalantly
admitting that the Goddess, as worshiped and
recognized in all the pagan cultures, was always

connected with the symbol of the snake, the dragon and chaos. Yet, Roberts does not admit this as a problem! Moreover, Roberts has also indicated that he is fully aware that the serpent who deceived Eve in the garden is, in reality, the power behind the great Mother Goddess. In his defiant book *From Eden to Eros*, he remarks:

> I must mention my visit to a planetarium, where by the miracle of a star projector and the courtesy of the director, I was transported back in time some six thousand years to the era of the Great Mother and saw the serpent rightfully restored to the pole. It was a moment of awe, for I was seeing the same divinities as did those who gazed above in 4000 B.C. . . . and I saw the serpent descend and ascend about the pole, reminding me of the spirit of life he brought to earth, and decent of my own spirit to earth, and its eventual return. And there, shining as his brightest eye, was the star known in Egypt as Isis, and Inanna in Babylonia, the Great Mother once more, all homage to her.[4]

Joseph Campbell, Roberts' associate, whose name became widely known after a PBS-TV series with Bill Moyers, likewise understood, yet embraced the secret behind the Goddess. In his bestselling four volume series *The Masks of God*, is revealed his knowledge of the serpent. Chapter One of the book by Campbell, *Occidental Mythology*, is entitled *The Serpent's Bride*. In it, Campbell writes: "The serpent who appeared and spoke to her (Eve) was a deity in his own right."[5]
Moreover, Campbell acknowledges the return, or the awakening of the Goddess, and the latter days activities of the serpent. Of the "great goddess of the universe," Campbell says that her return or rebirth is akin to "the moon sloughing her shadow, or the serpent sloughing its skin." Finally, Campbell makes the

shocking statement that the "Being of all beings" is the "serpent father." It is this serpent father, said Campbell, who is author of "an everlasting becoming."[6]

There's no way for the New Age to hide the obvious fact that it's a Satanic religion of the last days. The Bible clearly describes *who* the serpent is, and he is most definitely *not* the "Being of all beings" and a "deity in his own right:"

> And the great dragon was cast out, that old serpent, called the Devil, and Satan, which deceiveth the whole world (Revelation 12:9).

Will the Antichrist Bring a Spiritual Awakening?

New Age authorities such as Joseph Campbell, Richard Roberts, and others would not admit a belief in the devil, of course. They laugh and scoff at the very notion. Only the Christian fundamentalists believe in the devil, they would sneer. Yet, they invite us to pay homage to the Goddess. To respect the serpent father.

Another New Age authority, feminist theologian Mary Daly, has suggested that the Antichrist might not be something evil but *may instead be a sign of the awakening of the goddess* and the return of humankind to a matriarchal society.[7]

Daly questions "the idea that the Antichrist must be something evil." What if this is not the case as all, she asks. What if the idea has arisen out of the male's unconscious? She goes on to express her view that:

> The Antichrist dreaded by the Patriarchs may be the surge of consciousness, the *spiritual awakening*, that can bring us beyond Christ into a fuller stage of consciousness participating in the *living* God.

THE GODDESS AND THE SERPENT ☐ 157

Seen from this perspective the Antichrist and the
Second Coming of Women are synonymous. This
Second Coming is not a return of Christ but a new
arrival of female presence, once strong and powerful,
but enchained since the dawn of patriarchy . . .

The Second Coming then, means that the prophetic
dimension is the symbol of the Great Goddess . . .
(This) is the key to salvation.[8]

The startling truth is that in shaping themselves into
the image of the Great Goddess, *today's women are, in
reality, conforming themselves to the image which the
serpent, Satan, most desires them to become.* Ken Carey,
noted New Age spirit channeler, hints at this when he
seductively asks:

Why create yourself in the image of imperfection,
when the great spirit, source of all life, holds out to
you an image of unspeakable beauty?[9]

Carey's contention is that anything other than the
image of this "great spirit" would be an image of
imperfection. But who is the great spirit he is talking
about? Who is the hidden force behind the goddess?
Carey is prone to use such high sounding phrases as
"children of the light," "great spirit," "god's
consciousness," and "circle of the faithful of the stars."
But in one instance, buried deep on page 171 of his
book *Return of the Bird Tribes,* Carey discusses why his
"great spirit" has made earth his abode. He explains
that the climate range of this planet is one in which
"the beautiful child, the *Flying Winged One,* is created
and sustained."[10]
 Do we need really to ask Carey who is this *Flying
Winged One?* Do we not know that he is the *prince of*

the power of the air (Ephesians 2:2)? Could it be possible that Carey does not recognize the true identity of the one whom he worships? Or, is he simply writing in cryptic code phrases which are easily understood by the occult elite, but whose meaning is veiled from the masses?

The Rap of the Master Rapper

The spiritual messiah of the New Age, the one whom Carey describes as the "Flying Winged One," is just as active today as he was in the garden. There, he slyly became a "rapper," a master conversationalist who visited and communed with Eve. Unfortunately, instead of keeping her distance, she listened intently to him and was, finally, seduced by his smooth lies. Today, he comes to every woman with the very same lies. Probably, he's improved on his act with constant practice over the years. The vast majority of women have bought his lies. They have become imitations of Eve and modern-day Mystery Babylon goddesses. As such, they go about seducing other women and men into believing the lies of the serpent, just as Eve introduced Adam to the forbidden fruit.

The "You Can Become God" Lie

The most seductive New Age doctrine for modern woman and man is the deceptive lie that you "shall be as gods." This was the lie the serpent put in Eve's itching ears and it is still Satan's most effective weapon in the war to win souls from God.

I have yet to read the work of a New Age leader who does not believe in this destructive "man is an evolving god" heresy. F. Aster Barnwell expresses the mutually-held New Age view when he writes that the human being is "a God-seed, awaiting the conscious cooperation of the individual to awaken into full flowering." Twisting scripture, Barnwell claims that Jesus, Paul, and the Old Testament authors also taught that man is a god-in-becoming. He quotes the first of the Ten Commandments, "Thou shalt have no other God before me," alleging that the "me" is each of us. The Self, he says, is the "True God," implying that this commandment means that we should have no other gods outside ourselves.[11]

The twisting of God's Word is common among New Age ministers, teachers, and gurus. For example, The Maharishi Mahesh Yogi, founder of Transcendental Meditation (TM), interprets the statement in Psalms, "Be still and know that I am god," as meaning that every person should meditate and come to the realization that *he the individual* is God![12]

Elizabeth Clare Prophet, head of the Church Universal and Triumphant, which is claimed to have half-a-million active supporters, teaches that the White Brotherhood, the ascended Masters of Wisdom now in the spirit in the invisible dimension (Christians know them as demons), will help mankind realize that "we are gods." Their goal, she says, is to "provide every man and woman with the understanding of his own Christ Self, his own I Am Presence, and his status as a God-free being in this his own native universe."[13]

Again, we find a reference to--and a perversion of scripture. Prophet claims that this doctrine of man as god was given to the Brotherhood as the fulfillment of the prophecy of Jeremiah concerning the covenant which the Lord promised He would make with the House of Israel.

Prophet and other New Age leaders encourage their followers to practice spoken decrees in which they declare themselves to be God. Apparently, mind power and the individual's own "divine will" is expected to transform the decreeing person into a god. Prophet's suggested decree is partially as follows:

I Am the Presence of perfection
Living the Life of God in man!

All hail! I Am the living Christ
The ever-loving One
Ascended now with full God-power
I AM a blazing sun![14]

John Randolph Price recommends a similar decree be used during meditation in which the individual realizes his own Christhood and god-status. Among its phrases are these:

I begin with me.
I am a living soul and the Spirit of God dwells in me, as me.
I and the Father are one, and all that the Father has is mine.
In Truth I am the Christ of God.
Let Mankind be returned to Godkind . . .
It is done and it is so.[15]

From Eden to Babylon

Is this self-centered doctrine of "every women her own Goddess and Christ" a new revelation from God? Is it perhaps a holy fulfillment of biblical teaching, as

Elizabeth Clare Prophet maintains? The answer, most assuredly, is No! This hellish doctrine emanated from the serpent in Eden and later was an essential core teaching of Satan's Babylonian Mystery Religion. As Ralph Woodrow, in his excellent book, *Babylon Mystery Religion*, states:

> Looking back to the "Mother" of false religion--Babylon--we find that the people prayed to and honored a plurality of gods. In fact, the Babylonian system developed until it had some 5,000 gods and goddesses. . . . The Babylonians believed that their "gods" had at one time been *living heroes on earth*, but were now on a *higher plane*.[16]

In the Babylonian religion, Nimrod was the first of the man-gods, a mighty reincarnated soul whose own super will catapulted him to exalted status as God of gods and God of men. In Rome, the emperors were thought to be men-gods and in Egypt, the Mother Goddess Isis, almost a carbon copy of Babylon's Mother Goddess Semiramis, supposedly told her disciples, "I came of myself." In other words, with her creative powers, she willed herself into existence as the Goddess.[17]

The Babylonian religion and its imitators (including today's New Age) held in common a belief in reincarnation and karma. Through these processes, it was taught, the soul migrates toward godhood through successive reincarnations. However, superior willpower and ego strength can be employed to will oneself into godhood during a single life-span.

The Bible specifically warns against this arrogant doctrine. Jeremiah, whom, interestingly enough, New Age leader Elizabeth Clare Prophet lyingly claimed is the very source of her church's "man is god" philosophy, wrote these words from the Lord:

Thus shall ye say unto them, the gods that have not
made the heavens and the earth, even they shall
perish from the earth and from under these heavens
(Jeremiah 10:11).

Jeremiah also declared: "Thus saith the Lord;
cursed be the man that trusteth in man. . . . Blessed is
the man that trusteth in the Lord, and whose hope the
Lord is" (Jeremiah 17:5-7).

The New Age Call to Arms: "Reclaim Our Serpent Power!"

The New Age doctrine of rebirth, or spiritual awakening
and transformation, is often called *kundalini,* a hindu
term meaning *serpent power.* How appropriate! Satan
is described in the Bible as the serpent and it was in the
form of a serpent that he seduced Eve with his lies.
Now today, Satan comes to modern women with the
same lies. He soothingly insinuates that (1) they cannot
trust the God of the bible, (2) they can themselves
become gods, and (3) they will not die because of their
disobedience to God but will, instead, achieve
immortality through reincarnation and endless recycling
for an infinity.

Satan has not changed. He lied in the garden, he
lied at Babylon and now today, through his New Age
teachers, the Serpent's head arises once again, often in
a female form (the Goddess), spouting lies and
deceptions to the unwary.

It is no accident that a recent major New Age
magazine contained an article entitled "Reclaiming
Serpent Power." In the article, Alexandra Kovats, a
Catholic nun and former program director of Matthew

Fox's Institute in Culture and Creation Spirituality, wrote:

> In Hindu and Buddhist India the elevation of "Serpent Power," the *kundalini*, is a leading motif of yoga symbolism. It is the tantric image of the *female serpent* coiled in the base . . . of the spine.

> The aim of yoga is to rouse this serpent power, to lift *her* head and bring her up the channel of the spine to the . . . crown of the head. *She* is a symbol of transformation . . . as she moves up through the human body . . .

> Befriending this (serpent) creature can add to our own process of transformation. . . . Each of us must reclaim the power of the serpent . . . we can befriend the serpent to help us choose life and good . . .

> *I believe that it is time for us to reclaim the positive dimensions of serpent power in ourselves.*[18]

"Positive dimensions of serpent power?" Satan has so blinded the eyes of those in the New Age that they now follow after the Goddess fully knowing that she and her religion represent Lucifer, the serpent. To them, he is "positive," Jesus is "negative." Truly the "Strong Delusion" prophesied in II Thessalonians 2 is here! New Agers willingly embrace "The Lie." What's more, they demand that you and I do so as well. *Even so, come quickly Lord Jesus!*

TEN

The One Most Terrible Secret

Jesus answered and said unto him, Verily, verily, I say unto thee, Except a man be born again, he cannot see the Kingdom of God.

(John 3:3)

To invoke the Goddess is to awaken the Goddess within . . .

Miriam Starhawk
The Spiral Dance

There is a great and terrible secret that Satan's New Age leadership does not want you to know. That secret is the key to the incredible occurrences that are now transpiring throughout the world that so intensely affect every woman.

What is this great and terrible secret that the New Age has shrouded in darkness and kept hidden in the shadows? It is simply this: that the Goddess, whom Satan has created as a myth, *exists inside every woman.* Satan's great secret is that *each woman is to fully become an unholy incarnation of the Goddess.*

How is this to be accomplished? We know that the Bible tells us not to be transformed to the world but to be renewed in our minds. But the New Age operates on the opposite principle--the reverse of this godly doctrine. What Satan's New Age wants you to do is to become *just like the world.* You are to become like the Goddess. As a woman, you are literally and spiritually *to incarnate as the Goddess.*

Every Woman in the Image of the Goddess

It should really not surprise us that the New Age wants to mold you, I, and every other woman into the image of the Goddess. In Genesis we read that Adam and Eve were created in the image of God. God, in his love for us, still calls on you and I to be molded in his image. But now comes the New Age and its demonic forces with a counterfeit prescription for all of mankind. Women and men are to be made, conformed, transformed, remolded, remade and reshaped into the very image of the Goddess. This is the secret, the one most terrible secret the New Age does not want you to know.

The key, life-essential question for you is this: How far along has Satan come in succeeding with this goal in your life? In other words, *how far along are you toward being molded in the image of the Goddess?*

To help you answer this important question let us examine the mountainous evidence that it is indeed Satan's chief goal for women to mold each into the image of the goddess. After reviewing this astonishing evidence we will then take a look at that image itself. What is the image that Satan wishes to remold you into? What evil features comprise the makeup of the Goddess? Why would Satan and his New Age want every woman to be remolded in the express image of the Goddess? And finally, how does this reshaping of women fit in to Satan's grand scheme for world dominion in these, the last days?

Introducing the Goddess and Her Earth Religion

"We are on the threshold of the new Age of Aquarius, whom the greeks called . . . the water-bearer, the renewer, the reviver, the quencher of raging fire and of thirst."[1] These are the words of feminist Rosemary Ruether. Similar words have been echoed again and again by New Age teachers and leaders across the world. The Age of Aquarius, the time of the Goddess, they say, is once again here.

The ancient greeks depicted the Goddess as a woman carrying a pitcher of water which she pours onto the sacred ground of divine Earth to bring fertility and life to the planet. The Aquarian Age then, is the age of the water bearer, the woman, the Goddess.

Recently, in a major New Age magazine, *Gabriel's Horn*, the editors printed a poetic message from the "Father and Mother Gods." The message from the Mother God was most revealing:

> I am Mother. I am Daughter. I am the Earth vibration. I am whole and complete. I feed each soul with new life. I reconnect the body to the body of Mother Earth. I call to My babies to feed through Me. I am the Earth and I will nourish you in all your days.[2]

This message illustrates the spiritual lie of the New Age Goddess Religion. The call of this Mother Goddess to her "babies"--you and I and every other woman and man--*to feed through her* is significant.

We know of course that the New Age Goddess does not truly exist. She is but a myth, an imaginary creature of Satan which he implants in the minds of women and men everywhere to deceive them into believing that Mystery Babylon is desirable, holy and a worthy

Three modern-day images of the Goddess: (Top, left) The horned witchcraft goddess with her unicorn; (Top, right) A winged, Babylonian goddess; (Right) The goddess of fertility and magic, Celtic and Druid origins.

*Actress Kim Basinger (movie **Batman**) in goddess array--with lit candles and ivy wreath on head and flowing white gown. Below is an ad for a young girl's doll, wearing the same type garb.*

attainment. The "Goddess" is simply a synonym for "Satan." She is Satan cast in a feminine role.

For a woman to feed through the goddess (Satan) and to be nourished by her, it is necessary for what the New Age calls "incarnation of the goddess" to take place (In Christianity, we call this process by its true name: *demon possession!*). Ken Carey, a major New Age writer and spirit channeler, calls this the *incarnational process.* He says that incarnation occurs "when spirit beings consciously enter biological forms."

Carey further explains that this is the process of "awakening" in which a person achieves the maturing of his or her Higher Self.[3]

Letting Your Higher Self (a Demon) Take Charge of Your Life

It is important to understand what the New Age means by the phrase *Higher Self.* Basically, the New Ages teaches that each person is composed of a duality, of two parts: the Lower Self and a Higher Self (note the similarity of psychology's left brain/right brain theory). The goal of New Age incarnation is for the person to let this Higher Self (also called the "child within" or the "inner child") take charge.

In reality, the Higher Self is nothing more than a synonym for a demonic being. Thus, when a New Ager speaks of communicating with her Higher Self, she is simply stating that a demon spirit has possessed her and lives within! The individual is actually carrying on a relationship with this demonic spirit.

The despicable reality, then, is that, in the New Age, every woman is to receive a demonic spirit, the Higher Self, which will guide and lead that person into becoming the Goddess herself. This is the process called the *incarnation of the Goddess.*

This is Satan's counterfeit of what Christianity teaches through God's Word, the Holy Bible. If we believe in Jesus Christ and accept His precious gift of salvation, He will send the Holy Spirit to live within us. The Holy Spirit will guide us into all Truth. The New Age World Religion provides a counterfeit spirit. Once a person embraces the foul New Age doctrines, Satan sends one of *his* unholy spirits--demons--disingenuously called the "Higher Self," into the individual's flesh.

Satan literally incarnates through the individual, and begins to labor tirelessly to reshape that person into the image of the goddess. Remember: the Goddess is simply *the feminine version of Lucifer.* She is Satan's Mistress, the Mystery Woman, the devil in disguise.

The Two Women of Revelation: The Bride of Christ, The Bride of Satan

The book of Revelation talks about two women. One woman is depicted as the Church. She is the woman clothed with twelve stars with the son who will in time crush the very head of the serpent (Chapter 12). The second woman mentioned in Revelation is the Mystery Woman of Babylon, the Whore, the filthy entity (Revelation 17).

The first woman is the Bride of Christ, His Church, the redeemed. The second is literally the Bride of Satan, the unredeemed, the unrepentant, the unsaved, the rebellious who have rejected the one true God, Jesus Christ.

So we see pictured in Bible prophecy both the true Bride of Christ and the counterfeit Bride of Satan. Today,

Satan's New Age works furiously and tirelessly to capture an entire generation of women. His enslavement of woman is to be made complete through the incarnational process of the Goddess. In other words, Satan's goal is demonic possession and the takeover of the woman's soul. Women are to become incarnations of the Goddess.

As more and more people receive this incarnation of the Goddess, as they are remolded into her image and receive Goddess Consciousness, the entire world is being transformed into the New Age kingdom.

The New Age kingdom then, will not come to pass through some overnight miracle. Its success is a gradual process in which more and more people, especially women, are transformed into the Goddess nature. They take on the very characteristics of Satan. Most do so, however, without full knowledge of what is truly occurring. The Goddess Consciousness grows and grows in power and authority in their minds and souls. Finally, as spirit channeler and author Ken Carey writes:

> It continues to grow in strength and power and clarity until the very breast of mankind explodes in one great expression that is simultaneously both a longing and a rejoicing.[4]

According to Carey, the new frontier for mankind is not outer space but consciousness. The world needs "the gift of ourselves, he writes. "Awaken. Whole. Incarnate. . . ."[5] "Let our incarnations begin," Carey exclaims.[6]

Is God a Woman? Are We Her Daughters?

Z Budapest, a New Age supporter and witch who specializes in political issues, is in complete agreement with Carey. "The very essence of women's liberation," Budapest teaches, is that women understand "that God is a woman, and so are we, her daughters."

Budapest believes that all women must affirm the divine *within them*: "This practice of self-affirmation of the divine within us as women is, I believe, my most important contribution to modern witchcraft."[7]

How interesting that Budapest aligns witchcraft with this New Age goal of affirming the Goddess, the divine, within every woman.

Naomi Goldenberg, reporting on the first national All Woman Conference on Women's Spirituality, held in Boston almost a decade ago, wrote that women at the conference were advised to form *a mystical relationship* with Mother Nature and Mother Earth. They "were to keep a small altar in their homes to be used for meditation and for focusing their wills."[8]

According to Goldenberg the women were also advised to use mirrors on their altars to represent the Goddess. That way each time they looked in the mirror they would be reminded not only that there is a Goddess who represents them, but that they are in the very image of the Goddess. And like the Goddess, they too possess divine beauty, power and dignity.[9]

Anyone who has studied the occult for even a limited amount of time will understand the deeper meaning of what Goldenberg and the many other New Age authorities are teaching. What is really at stake here is the soul of the individual. To become like the Goddess, to fully incarnate as the woman described in Revelation 17 as "Mystery, Babylon," is to be possessed by demonic spirits from the pit of hell.

Of course, the New Ager does not experience it as demon possession. For example, in her TV special promoting the New Age, actress Shirley MacLaine sits in a pool of bubbling, steamy water. An incredible feeling comes over her, she confesses. It's happening, an incredible oneness with nature, with the universe. She is experiencing what Hindus call the Ultimate Reality.

MacLaine feels a blissful and positive energy force run through her body; then, through astral travel, she has an out-of-body experience. In effect, this transcendent feeling in which the self vanishes or diminishes and dissolves into and becomes one with the whole, is an excellent description of demon possession. The New Age calls it *transformation*. They even use the term *born again*, *holistic*, or *metamorphosis*. However, any Christian who truly knows what being *born again* (see John 3:3) means realizes the horrendous truth. The satanic counterfeit of God's being born again is a uniquely unholy experience.

Shirley MacLaine and all of the others who become "one with the universe" in effect have become *one with the devil*. They have achieved a close encounter of the worst kind. They have become the Goddess. Again, I emphasize that *the Goddess is simply Satan in another form*. It is his feminine disguise.

The Secret Doctrine and Initiation

It has been the goal of Mystery religions through the eons of time for man and woman to become "one" with the Goddess--to allow "her" to fully take over the mind and the body. The Mystery religions of Babylon and their successors taught this as the *secret initiation*. Today in the New Age we see the rebirth of this hideous ancient, yet perennial, doctrine. It is a doctrine that promises the keys to the tree of life. It is held out to be the path to godhood for woman and man. The New Age teaches that only when a woman or a man becomes one with "god" or to be more precise, one with the Goddess, does a person become whole and divine.

What has actually been accomplished in this union with the Goddess is that the person's spirit and flesh become harlots in common with the Whore of Babylon. The forbidden fruit has been plucked from the tree. Sensual cravings have been stirred deep within. It is, say the mysticists, the dark journey of the soul that has been traveled.

Inviting the Darkness into One's Soul

While the word "darkness" is abhorred by the biblical Christian, it is seen as a word of strength and attractiveness to the average New Ager. New Age leaders such as Matthew Fox and others see the darkness as something desirable. It is a place where mystical gifts are received. "Mysticism," says Fox, "takes us into the darkness of what Carl Jung (the occult psychiatrist) calls the lavishing mother." Fox highly advises his followers to accept "the mystical invitation to be with the darkness."[10]

To Fox and others the darkness *is* God incarnate. And since the New Age teaches that each of us is an extension of God, we are also each an extension of darkness. Thus, to invite the Goddess within is to invite the darkness into our souls. Through darkness, we become *one* with God. Therefore we *become* God. As the spirits told New Age writer Ken Carey:

> Each of us is an extension of God. It is we, who as it is recorded created man after *our* image and after *our* likeness. For thousands of years, humans have been afraid of us. Many of them are now learning that they have nothing to lose and everything to gain by establishing contact with us once again.[11]

Carey teaches that intelligences from another realm wish to communicate and merge with us. They are God, he says, and they want us to know that we, too, are God. In reality, they are *demonic beings* who wish to merge with--that is, possess--mankind.

Ken Carey provides an explanation of what this merger involves. He explains that his extraterrestrial visitors wish to *incarnate* into human beings. He quotes them as saying:

> Not until these closing years of the twentieth century have we been able to incarnate fully and completely, aligning our spiritual bodies with the physical, etheric, mental and emotional bodies of not just one woman or one man here or there, but with many, at times even whole communities.[12]

Carey's visitors told him that there is today an explosion of "consciousness" in the world. They boast that people are once again turning to the "Great Spirit" who is the source of all information: "Our spirits incarnate in ever growing numbers . . . truth spreads. And how beautiful it is!"[13]

The message these demonic visitors impart to us is that we should welcome and invite them into our awareness: "Make a home for eternal spirit in your heart," they remarked. If you do, you will "become one with God:"

> You are all God beings in potential with no reason not to become God beings in reality. Trust yourself.[14]

When you trust *yourself*, you are trusting God, these spirits from Satan's realm suggest. What liars! They well know that once you begin to rely only on yourself, you are trusting Satan, the "god" who lives within you. This is the incarnational process.[15]

By Whatever Name It is Called, It is Demon Possession

To be molded into the image of the Goddess also is described by New Agers as a process of *integration*. One New Ager calls it *psychosynthesis*. Another, *individuation*. And then another, *self-realization*. But whatever term is used, it's clear the process is the same. I feel it imperative to emphasize once again that to become an incarnation of the Goddess--to be molded in her image-- is to become *demon-possessed*. It is Satan's ultimate goal to possess every woman and every human being. It is a goal he has already achieved with millions of people, and many more are to come in these last days.

Satan considers women merely as lambs for the slaughter. Leonardo Boff, a New Age-oriented priest, describes woman as the *container*. "The key symbol of the feminine," writes Boff, "is the container, the receptacle." He notes that any container or receptacle has an inside *and* an outside. Likewise, a woman has a body *and* a spirit. This body and spirit, Boff explains, experience things inside and outside. Therefore, inside each woman, he remarks, there is a "mysterious deep and dark" dimension. To confront that dimension, says Boff, is "to assimilate it and surrender to it."[16]

Again we see the New Age call to women to surrender to the darkness, to the shadows. Carl Jung, the occult psychiatrist so admired by New Agers today, called this the *containment of individuation*. Jung believed that when a woman or man achieves *holism*--when the individual incorporates the shadow or the darkness into his or her personality--that person holistically becomes one. The "eternal feminine" is achieved.[17]

Alcoholics Anonymous (AA) and the Goddess Religion

These same unholy teachings are being spread today through Alcoholics Anonymous (AA) and other twelve step groups. AA, Al-Anon, the Adult Children of Alcoholics, and other twelve step programs have bought fully the New Age doctrines of the Higher Self, integration, psychosynthesis and individuation, as defined by Carl Jung and other occultists.

For example, in the book *Guide to Recovery*, a guide for Adult Children of Alcoholics, authors Herbert Gravitz and Julie Bowden discuss the concept of the Higher Self. They explain that a higher level of consciousness is attained through one's Higher Self.

Moreover, they state that the chief goal of Alcoholics Anonymous is to assist the individual to become whole--to become one--with the Higher Self. This is, they say, the pathway to "spiritual evolution." Those who walk the path of the twelve step programs of Alcoholics Anonymous, Al-Anon, Overeaters Anonymous, and so forth travel the "spiritual road" which assures a "genesis" or an "awakening":

> Genesis (rebirth) is . . . the spiritual awakening spoken of in Alcoholics Anonymous; you begin to be aware of a spiritual connection which unites us all in a sense of being one with the universe.[18]

Keep in mind that AA's "spiritual awakening" does not make you a Christian, nor does a 12-stepper have to believe in and accept Jesus as Lord. According to AA and other twelve step programs, the healed and spiritually mature person "awakens" to her oneness with the universe. This is New Age religion *par excellence*. It is union with the spirit of the Goddess, which AA prefers to describe as connecting with one's "higher power" or "god as you understand him."

The Bible does not connect us with some hazy and nebulous "higher power." Nor does man have the option of selecting his own god--"god as you understand him." The True God, as revealed in the Bible, has a name: Jesus. He is understood by reading His Word.

Does Holy Sex Awaken the Goddess Within?

Likewise, the practice of *tantra--that is sexual--yoga* is involved with the person being able to incarnate as the Goddess. Through sexual ritual, it is claimed that a woman becomes aware of, communicates with, and is guided by the Higher Self (demonic powers).

Tantric sex is not unique to the New Age. It has been practiced for centuries and was commonplace in the Mystery religions and in Hinduism. As world religions expert Geoffrey Parrinder explains:

> Tantra was the rediscovery of the mystery of woman, for every woman became an incarnation of the *shakti*, the divine woman and mother. . . . For tantra the greatest energy was sexual, and the sexual organs represented cosmic powers . . .

> Sexual intercourse of any kind was treated in a ritual fashion, between husband and wife, or different partners, or with a temple girl. Sexual union was transformed into a ceremonial rite through which the human couple became a divine pair.[19]

Sex, then, is clearly believed by the New Age and taught by Satan as an important pathway to becoming the

Goddess. Through divine sexual intercourse (tantric sex) it is believed by the Hindus and New Agers of yesterday *and today* that a man and a woman--or for that matter a man and a man or a woman and a woman--can attain spiritual ecstasy and divinity. Unusual powers can be acquired if the sex act is conducted with the Goddess in mind.

As we have discovered, the word *yoga* itself means to be *yoked with the Goddess*. Thus, tantric yoga literally means to invite the Goddess within or to be yoked with her. Through sacred sex, the partners unite and come into complete harmony with the mystery woman represented as Satan's Goddess. Miriam Starhawk, one of the world's best known witches, has stated that the act of sexual intercourse *awakens* the Goddess. Her teaching is that the Goddess comes forth at the most intense and rapturous moment of orgasm, and enters the couple.[20]

The word *awakening* is a popular one among New Age teachers. As his spirit guides told Ken Carey, "your race is soon to experience widespread *awakenings*, or as some will see it, a massive descent of beings from the stars."[21]

It is no mistake, then, that Alcoholics Anonymous and other twelve step programs as well as the practicers of tantric sex, uniformly speak of an *awakening* that occurs. That awakening is, in effect, the acceptance of the Goddess into the human being. An awakening happens when a person *is possessed* by the Goddess. Or, better stated, a person is possessed by *demons* who slavishly endeavor to remold the individual into the Goddess image desired by their master, Satan.

ELEVEN

Initiation: The Seduction of Women

For they are the spirits of devils, working miracles, which go forth unto the kings of the earth and of the whole world to gather them . . .

(Revelation 16:14)

We come to the earth to blend with you in the communion that will give you birth. . . . We offer you ourselves.

"incarnating spirits," in Ken Carey's
Return of the Bird Tribes

The popular notion of demonic possession, inspired by thriller movies and fantasy horror novels, is that it happens all at once. Suddenly a demon spirit appears on the scene, hungrily enters a person's soul, and takes total command. But this is not usually the pattern of possession. Most often Satan acquires influence slowly in the person's life. Initially invited by a woman's unholy lifestyle or by her dabbling in occultism or the New Age, demonic forces conquer the individual step-by-step in an *initiation process*. The end result of this journey to the shadowlands is New Age transformation, or rebirth.

The Counterfeit Rebirth of Satan's New Age

Awakening the Goddess within therefore occurs through a process of *initiation*. Initiation is similar to the Christian concept of regeneration. The New Age teaches that through initiation a person reaches a peak experience level by which rebirth occurs. Some speak of this as the "awakening of the Goddess" within while other New Agers describe this as the arousal and awakening of the *kundalini serpent power* in the spine. Many take note of a bright light that seems to explode with staggering intensity inside the brain, bringing on incredible heights of ecstasy and a warm feeling of being simultaneously bathed by a thousand sensitive hands: the hands of the Goddess.

Here again we see the counterfeit of Satan. We know that rebirth as a Christian--to be *born again*--is a supreme experience in which the born again person is transformed and becomes totally renewed (John 3:3; John 3:16). A born again Christian woman receives the Spirit of God, a joyous experience that is so wonderfully magnificent that no words can describe it.

When Satan comes along with his cheap and shoddy imitation achieved through initiation, the end result is incarnation of the Goddess within the woman. The major difference, of course, is that the Satanic regeneration never satisfies. For once a demon possesses a woman, insatiable lusts and carnal and material desires dictate every moment of her existence. She becomes a slave to Satan. As she is molded into the Goddess, she wants more and more and more of what the Goddess has to offer. She never gets enough. Like Jezebel of the Bible, she beds again and again and again with sin, becoming the Whore over and over, yet she is never satisfied. Endlessly and restlessly she searches for something "more," but finds only distress, agony, and despair. Momentary feelings of joy and contentment invariably evaporate and dissolve into nothingness.

How to be Possessed by the Goddess Spirit

There are a variety of methods, practices, and techniques through which a woman can become incarnated and possessed by the Goddess Consciousness or spirit. For example, Starhawk writes that rhythm and music accompanied by chanting and body movement is one pathway to the Goddess:

> Rhythm, whether experienced in motion, song, drumming, chanting, or poetic meter, also induces a state of heightened awareness. Afro-American religions depend heavily on rhythmic drumming and dancing to induce a trance state in which worshippers become 'mounted' or possessed by the gods. The metrical rhythm of poetry . . . induces a trance of heightened sensitivity . . . certain rhythms induce particular emotional states. . . . Spoken trance inductions are always soft, sing-song and rhythmic.[1]

Evidently, intense female fantasies of an impure or sinful nature can also bring on the goddess. This is possible only after a woman has continuously and over a long period of time allowed her mind to degenerate through unholy thoughts and carnal desires. Starhawk, for example, stresses that "day dreaming" can bring on a trance as the mind tunes into an etheric, spirit-realm channel and allows an entity to form within.

The New Age would have us believe that the Goddess is always resident inside--that she only needs to be *awakened.* New Age teachers say that if we can only gain the knowledge of her existence and take action to awaken her she will come alive and become an integral and inseparable part of us forever. We can do so simply by invoking, or inviting, her presence, or by visualizing her coming. As Starhawk explains:

> To invoke the Goddess is to awaken the Goddess within, to
> become . . . that aspect we invoke. An invocation channels
> power through a visualized image of Divinity.[2]

Starhawk goes on to explain, "We are already one with
the Goddess--she has been with us from the beginning, so
fulfillment becomes. . .a matter of self awareness. For
women, the Goddess is the symbol of the inmost self. She
awakens the mind and spirit and emotions. Through her
we can know the power of our anger and aggression as
well as the power of our love."[3]

We Are the Goddess, So Protect Mother Earth

According to New Age theology, each woman is the
Goddess. She needs only awaken the Goddess within.
Now, the New Age also teaches that the Goddess is the
planet Earth, Mother Earth, or Gaia. She is both the
earth and us, so we are interconnected with the Earth.
This is the reason, then, for the New Age emphasis on
ecology and environment. They wish to protect Mother
Earth, the Goddess, of whom they believe they are a part.

If all we are are parts of the whole, parts of the
Goddess, then certainly no one has a direct line on Truth.
Jesus, Buddha, Muhammad, Moses--no one has a corner
on the Truth. We all come from the Earth. We are all
equal although some are at higher progressions of divinity.

According to New Age religious teachings, the
pathway to wisdom, to truth, is the Goddess. Therefore,
we can all become "Christs." We can all be God, for we
are already parts of God. To connect with the God Force
it is only necessary to awaken the Goddess within.

Starhawk gives the traditional New Age view of how
we are connected to the Goddess and to the entire
universe as follows:

We are the Goddess. We are each a part of the inter
penetrating, inter connecting reality that is all.

The Goddess, the divine, is immanent in the world,
manifest in nature, in human beings, in human community.
The All That Is One is not now and never has been
separate from this existing physical world. She is here
now, *is* each of us in the eternal changing present; is no
one but you, is no where but where you are--and yet is
everyone.

To worship her is to assert . . . that life is good, a great gift,
a constant opportunity for ecstasy.[4]

The New Age teaching is that the Goddess is not out
there but instead she is *in* everything and she *is* everything
and we are part of her. Thus, Starhawk declares:

Mother Goddess is reawakening, and we can begin to
recover our primal birthright, the sheer, intoxicating joy of
being alive. We can open new eyes and see that there is
nothing to be saved *from*, no struggle of life against the
universe, no god outside the world to be feared and
obeyed, only the Goddess, the Mother, the turning spiral
that whirls us in and out of existence, whose winking eye is
the pulse of being--birth, death, rebirth. . . . Who is found
only through love: love of trees, of stones, of sky and
clouds, of scented blossoms and thundering waves . . .
through love of ourselves . . . each of us our own star, Her
child, Her lover, Her beloved, Her Self.[5]

This coincides, of course, with the Satanic doctrine
that God is *a force* rather than a person who loves each of
us. This force, the Goddess doctrine, says Starhawk and
other New Agers, is "The feminist religion of the future."[6]
In reality, it is more than just a feminist religion, it is a
religion for all--for all men and women who reject the

true Lord and Savior, Jesus Christ. The Goddess truly has awakened.

The Worship of Nature

In this New Age Goddess Religion, nature is worshiped. Oneness with nature, and oneness and unity with the universe is said to lead to a Goddess Consciousness on the part of men and women. This is why the transcendent experience of oneness, the experience of moving beyond oneself and encompassing the entire universe, becoming part of the All, is the common denominator among New Agers.

As I have said, this is, in reality, demon possession. But the experience is so phenomenal--it is so intensely special and delightful to New Agers--that they become convinced that a heavenly form of energy has enveloped them. This is how one New Ager described her experience of being transformed into this sense of oneness, this union with the Goddess Consciousness:

> This led to an experience of illumination, a mystical experience of oneness and unity and light." I was out walking one morning and felt suddenly uplifted. I remember I knew timelessness, spacelessness and lightness. There were no people or even animals around but every flower, every bush, every tree seemed to wear a halo. There was a light emanation around everything and flecks of gold fell like slanted rain through the air.

> The important part of it was the realization of the oneness of all creation. . .a oneness with that which permeates all and binds all together and gives life to all.

I had received the first glimpse of what the life of inner peace was like . . .it was a point of no return. I found I could . . . never again feel separate.[7]

This ecstatic experience soon, however, fades and is replaced by an uneasy, empty feeling of anxiety. Of course, it is Satan's big lie to tell us that there is no way out of our difficulty. That we cannot escape our dilemma once we have accepted the path of the New Age Goddess. The Bible tells us otherwise. God hears our pleas. If we turn to him with a sincere spirit and with repentance in our heart, with brokenness and need and a desire to be cleansed and to serve him, he will hear our pleas and our cry for help. We do not have to remain "separate" from God. We do not have to be enslaved to Satan and his New Age. We can be free, free for eternity.

Enslavement of Women by the New Age

While Jesus Christ and Christianity offer freedom and liberty, the New Age Goddess offers chains and bondage. As a woman is remolded and fashioned into the image of the Goddess she becomes vulnerable and susceptible to demonic forces. Through sin and rejection of God, today's average woman is enthusiastically and blindly embracing the New Age. Often she does not realize this. But the world is so polluted with New Ageism that the Goddess cannot be held back by one's own will or by natural means. Only the supernatural defenses of Jesus Christ can help a woman to withstand the ravages of the New Age system.

Wherever we turn, in medicine and economics, in education, entertainment, the media, television, radio, women's magazines, and, regrettably, even in many church pulpits today, women confront Satan's New Age. Things do not always come labeled New Age. They are not always easily recognized as New Age. But nevertheless, the New Age influence is there, whether a woman knows it or not. Like waves of the ocean and tides that slowly erode away a coastline, New Ageism gradually but surely erodes a woman's moral fiber and leaves her open to attack by demonic forces of the Goddess.

Demon Spirits on the Prowl

The Bible prophesies that in the last days, a strong delusion will fall on all of humanity. Those who have rejected the Truth will be drawn irresistibly and unavoidably toward the Lie, the strong delusion of Satan (II Thessalonians 2).

Kenneth Carey quotes his spirit guides as stating, "we of the winged tribes arrive in this age not just to materialize, but to *incarnate*. We are coming back at this time on a wave of light, a pulsation of new intensity . . ."[8]

Did you note the words "winged tribes?" Isn't it interesting that although we do not know the exact form of the entities known as Satan's dark angels, these demons describe themselves as winged tribes. Possibly they do have what would appear to be, or are, wings of angels. In any case, here is what these demonic entities say they are looking for as they travel the earth realm hungrily prowling for women's bodies to possess and devour:

> We are looking for biological incarnations in the specific human beings whose present bodies have grown from fetuses that have unfolded along the vibrational patterns of our light . . . let us wake up in you . . . you, whose physical circuitry mirrors our being; welcome us into your consciousness.[9]

It is apparent that these demon spirits want to merge with women and men today. They go on to state:

> When you experience our spirit presence, you know yourself in the image that God holds for you, the image of perfection in which God has created you . . . we are designed to blend with your consciousness, with your understanding.

> We come to the earth to blend with you in the communion that will give birth. . . . Our love has called up out of the earth the bodies of your race. Feel that love and know your spirit. We offer more than words. We offer you ourselves.[10]

Yes indeed, they do offer you themselves. These demons want you to invite them in. They want you to willingly and eagerly accept the blending process, to become the Goddess incarnate, Satan's woman. Naturally they come as angels of light, for Paul himself told us in the Bible that Satan's ministers of unrighteousness often come disguised as angels of light. This is why these demon spirits--the winged tribe--want us to believe that they come as our help-mates. If we would just allow them in, if we would incarnate them into our very being, there is so much, they claim, they could do for us:

> We are here to calm the troubled waters of . . . emotional storms . . . to bring the ways of love to a human world tossing still in a troubled sea of illusion. We bring the torch of peace . . . we bring the torch of wisdom that resolves human differences through . . . forgiveness, honesty.[11]

These spirits from the Adversary that seek to blend with you know Satan's one most terrible secret. Therefore, they lie and deceive by proclaiming that they come in love, honesty, caring, and compassion. If you accept their lie, in other words, if you live for the world, if your thoughts and actions mirror Satan's world, for he is, the Bible says, the god of this world, then you will inevitably become an authentic imitation of the Goddess. As the demon spirits who came to Ken Carey so aptly put it, *"moment by moment you become more incarnate."*[12]

They Want an Entire Generation

Yes, you can become the Goddess incarnate. You can invite her in. The winged tribes want you to know that they are always in waiting. As a matter of fact, if you have not accepted Jesus Christ today they stand at the door impatiently awaiting your invitation. But they do not knock and patiently plead like our Lord Jesus; often they barge right in and attempt to overcome your sensibilities and invade your mind:

> We seek to awaken in your minds and hearts, to incarnate in your bodies . . . we do not evolve, we incarnate.[13]

You are not the only chosen victim of Satan's demonic forces. He wants an entire generation! Ken Carey was told that:

> The Circle of the Faithful of the Stars was invited to incarnate *en masse* as a single global generation . . . we would enter human forms, some to incarnate in the next wave of children and others in their children's children.[14]

Although demons are prone to lies and enjoy deceptions more than almost anything else, the fact is, the Bible does tell us that in the last days Satan will be furious because he knows his time is short. The pit will loose the spirits which now are bound, God having sent an angel down from heaven with keys to open wide the door. Evidently, in the last days millions of additional dark angels are to be released onto planet earth to plague humanity. They will bring in the end times and eventually the return of our Lord.

We know that Jesus Christ will put an end to their evil, as he sets up His Kingdom (Revelation 19-22); but for now they roam, practically unrestrained, though they cannot touch the few who are God's children without His permission.

Thus, it is not an idle boast that these demons insist that they were invited, obviously by their master, Lucifer, to incarnate in the bodies of human beings *en masse* and to take over almost an entire global generation. However, note that they themselves confess that even if they are not able to capture an entire generation at once, then one wave of them will succeed in taking many children in this generation--then the next wave, their children's children.

Texe's book, *Ravaged by the New Age: Satan's Plan to Destroy our Kids*, is certainly testimony to the fact that Satan has made our children a prime target today. He is an impatient master. But he realizes that it is necessary to first win over the hearts and minds of the mothers of this generation. Women have the highest priority. Through the women, Satan knows he can then go on to capture their children, their husbands, their friends and loved ones.

It has been said that the hand that rocks the cradle rules the world. This is no doubt true. Satan well understands this human relations principle. He therefore is in heavy pursuit of the hands that rock the cradles. Women, I am convinced, are the chief target today for the demonic invasion. We women are the ones that Satan most seeks to incarnate in. His evil goal is to massively seduce our entire generation of women.

The horrible facts indicate that Satan is well along in this diabolical, almost breathtaking, yet disgusting goal. The Goddess has made great strides. And, now she stands radiantly in her flowing white gown, her blond hair streaming in the wind, her blue eyes gleaming as she unfolds her arms and invites every woman to enter therein.

TWELVE

You, Too, Can Become a Goddess

Beloved . . . ye should earnestly contend for the faith which was once delivered to the saints. For there are certain men crept in unawares . . .

(Jude 1:3-4)

The New Age is upon us and we are witnessing the birth pains of the new culture and the civilization. That which is old and undesirable must go.

Alice Bailey
Lucis Trust

How does one become a goddess? The answer lies in our discovery of who the Goddess is. We have already noted that Revelation 17 pictures the Goddess as the mystery woman, the whore, of Babylon. Therefore, if we wish to understand what kind of image Satan and his New Age wish to shape you and every other woman in, we simply need to further examine the Goddess of Babylon and her followers.

The Goddess of Babylon, first known as Semiramis and later as Inanna, Astarte, Ishtar, Ashtoreth, and by other names, initiated her followers into the Mysteries. Today,

New Age leaders also desire that women be initiated into the Mysteries:

> These ancient Mysteries were originally given to humanity by the Hierarchy. . . . The Mysteries will be restored. Everything is being rapidly brought to the surface. . . . Our church organizations, with their limiting and confusing theologies, will give place to the Hierarchy, with its emerging teaching. . . . The Masters know exactly that which must be done, by right timing.

> The New Age is upon us and we are witnessing the birth pains of the new culture and the civilization. That which is old and undesirable must go.[1]

Alice Bailey is correct. The Mysteries *have* been restored by the New Age, for the New Age is a Mystery Religion. The Goddess who represents the New Age has come to initiate every woman who is not a follower of Jesus Christ into her Mysteries:

> Hear the words of the Star Goddess, the dust of whose feet are the host of heaven, whose body encircles the universe.

> I who am the beauty of the green earth. . . . I call upon your soul to arise and come unto me. For I am the soul of nature that gives life to the universe. From Me all things proceed and unto Me they must return. Let My worship be in the heart that rejoices, for behold--all acts of love and pleasure are My rituals . . . and you who seek to know Me know that your seeking and yearning will avail you not, unless you know the Mystery . . . for behold, I have been with you from the beginning, and I am that which is attained at the end of desire.[2]

It is frightening but true that many women do desire to be shaped in the image of the Goddess. As one prominent New Age teacher has proclaimed, "the symbolism of the Goddess has taken on an electrifying power for modern women."[3]

The Goddess has great appeal for today's would-be goddesses--women of the New Age.

The vast majority of women today are easy prey for the New Age and have absolutely no resistance to the forces that are being exerted upon them. In her book, *Esoteric Psychology I*, Alice Bailey bragged about the New Ages success in shaping women into the New Age mold. She observed that, "for the first time in racial history, we have the expression of a true human being."

"We have," said Bailey, "the personality, integrated and functioning as a unit, and we have the mind and the emotional nature fused and blended, on the one hand with a physical body, and on the other with the soul."[4]

It is interesting that this top New Age leader acknowledges that the Goddess Movement, which is the New Age, has such an intractable grasp on the personality, the mind, the emotions, the physical body or the flesh, and the soul of so many women. Judging from the conduct and behavior of most women today, Alice Bailey's boast was not an idle one.

Alice Bailey also has stated that the New Age is bringing an inflow of energy that possesses "transforming power and regenerating force"[5] It is because of this occult power and force, wrote Bailey, that the New Age is able to accurately make this claim: "we have mankind in a condition where the response to the deeper spiritual energies and to the new opportunities is, for the first time adequate." Because of this, she writes, the New Age has a "great day of opportunity. Hence the wonder of the dawn which can be seen brightening in the east."[6]

The Religious Seduction of Women

Over the last few decades, Satan has easily been able to maneuver women into a position today in which they have fully bought into the New Age religious system. In every family in America today at least one member or another is involved in some type of New Age activity.

What is a New Age activity? In Chapter 6 we listed a number of the techniques, practices, rituals and doctrines of the New Age common among women today. Here again is just a sampler:

Astrology

Mysticism

Sorcery

Inner Healing

Crystal Powers

Mental Imagery

New Age Music

Human Potential

Higher Power

Lesbianism

Color Therapy

Astral Travel

Animism

Divination

The Third Eye

Levitation

Ecstatic Dancing

Visualization

Karma

Holistic Health

Spirit Channeling

The Mythologies

Globalism

Higher Self

Magic/Magick

Ultra-feminism

Biofeedback

Trance States

Cartomancy

Fortune Telling

Psychokinesis

Self-esteem

Sacred Sex

Shamanism

Reincarnation

Yoga

Psychic Powers

UFOs

Chanting

Witchcraft

False Bibles

Amulets

Hypnosis

Idolatry

Iridology

Tarot Cards

Telepathy

Self-love

Medieval Fantasy Novels

Cosmic Consciousness

The Peace Movement

Magical Charms

Nature/Earth Worship

Out-of-the-Body Exieriences

Demon Speaking in Tongues

Counterfeit Signs and Wonders

Altered States of Consciousness

Symbols (unicorn, pyramid, horn of plenty, lightning
bolt, pentagram star, etc.)

Transcendental Meditation

Higher Consciousness

The Prosperity Gospel

ESP/Psychic Powers

Positive Thinking/Confession

Occult Books and Literature

Alcohol/Mind Altering Drugs

All of the things listed above are prevalent in the New Age World Religion. If we could travel back in time to ancient Babylon, or if we take the time to study the history of Babylon as revealed through archeological findings, we discover that every one of these were practiced in Babylon centuries before Jesus was born. The restoration of these Mystery practices and beliefs is astonishing. It provides definitive proof that Mystery Babylon, the religion of Satan, has come full circle. The Goddess is back. And she has brought with her all of the filth and fornication that the priests and priestesses of Babylon first invented with the help of Satan's dark angels in the ancient days of that great city.

Sale of Goddess jewelry is booming, as these recent ads demonstrate (addresses of firms deleted).

Want to be a Goddess? . . . Live Like the Devil

Becoming the Goddess, allowing her to enter into and conquer your soul, is not, however, only a matter of religious practices. There are many thousands of women today who are in the image of the Goddess simply because of the unholy lifestyles they have chosen. As the cigarette commercial says, "You've come a long way, baby." The problem is, where have you gone? Which path have you traveled down? Only a tiny minority of women have taken

the road less traveled which Jesus identified as the narrow
way and the straitgate which few enter therein. Instead,
most have taken the broad path of destruction. Once we
reject Jesus Christ and his truth then we cannot help being
led by the spirit of deception along pathways that are
destructive and dangerous.

We can understand the lifestyle which Satan's New
Age wants women to follow if we but look at the ancient
lifestyle of the women who were followers of the Goddess
in ancient Babylon and also women who worship, adored,
and patterned their lives after the ancient goddesses of
Egypt, Greece, and Rome. Once again we travel back in
time and what we find is fascinating.

The picture of the women of those days who were
understudies and admirers of the Goddess amazingly
resembles that of women today. The model of the ancient
Goddess was that of a desirable, lusty, sensuous and carnal
woman who in a split moment could change and become
nurturing mother, protector, and compassionate overseer.
On one hand she alluringly gave her body to men; on the
other hand she would often hold her body back until a
man gave her what she asked for. What she asked for
could well be money, a gift of great value, or literally the
mind, body and soul of the seeker.

In a sense, the Goddess was much like her master,
lover and consort, Satan. She could alternatively be
aggressive or passive, tempting or withdrawing. Never
however, was the Goddess pictured as being dependent
on men. Instead, she was always superior to men, who
were cast in a subordinate role. The Goddess was
Supergirl, Superwoman, Wonderwoman, Amazon,
Delilah, Temptress, Dominatrix. Never a co-dependent,
she was strong, empowered with unusual supernatural
power and psychic forebodings. She was crafty, wise, all-
knowing.

The Queen Bee and Her Worker Bees

The Goddess was able to entrance her male and female subjects and draw them into her domain with some kind of irresistible sex magic. As the queen bee, the workers of the hive were to serve her. Yet, in so doing, they received from her an ample abundance of honey. Perhaps the honey bee is the best symbol of the Goddess. This was, in fact, one of the symbols of the ancient Goddess.

It is interesting that Ralph Waldo Emerson, the famed educator who also was a New Ager, wrote an ode to the bee:

> The humble Bee. Wiser far than human seer. Yellow-breached philosopher! Seeing only what is fair, sipping only what is sweet, dothest mock at fate and care, leave the shaft and take the wheat.

The Mother Goddess was considered the Queen Bee by her subjects, pagan worshippers.

In his bestselling book about UFOs and aliens, *Communion*, Whitley Strieber described the ones who abducted him as being led by a mystery woman who perfectly fit the description of the Mother Goddess of Babylon. "She was," said Strieber, "ruthless, determined." Serving her was a group of male subjects whom Striber compared to bees in a hive.[7]

It is prophetically significant that in the Old Testament, when Samson fought, conquered, and killed the savage lion, from the carcass of the lion appeared a colony of bees. The lion has long represented the unknown god, Lucifer, of the Babylonian religion. When Samson killed the lion and within its carcass the bees appeared, what we have pictured is an analogy to Revelation 13. There we see that the Beast who will arise from the sea in the last days will have seven heads. But one of these heads will be wounded as if to death. Similarly, the lion slain by Samson could have been symbolic of the Lion of the East, the Babylonian occult system.

Note that the Beast, Samson's lion, was apparently slain, yet from its depths sprang a hive of honey bees. Could this be a picture of the wounded Goddess coming back restored to vigorous, revived life in the last days?

Recently in our ministry we came upon some literature from the Fort Worth, Texas Independent School District. On the front cover of one particular brochure, there were three symbols configured together: the earth globe, a triangle, and the bee. The literature itself did not explain what these symbols meant but realizing that Maria Montessori, the founder of the Montessori method now in such widespread use in schools, was an occultist, a Theosophist, and a New Ager, we can easily discern what these symbols mean.

We are simply seeing here a representation and an image of Satan's unholy trinity (or *triangle*): Mother Goddess (the Queen Bee), Father of Light (which is he, Lucifer) and Antichrist, the Son of Perdition (see II

202 □ NEW AGE LIES TO WOMEN

Thessalonians 2), all conspiring to take command of planet earth. The honey bee, which represents the Mother Goddess, is how they plan to do it. The Queen Bee is to inspire her worker bees to go forth and harvest the crop of humanity, bringing in the honey, the nectar, so that the New Age Kingdom can have sustenance and power.

Do You Qualify for the Cult of the Mother Goddess?

Do you qualify as a member of the cult of the Mother Goddess? Have you, unsuspectingly and perhaps unwittingly, allowed yourself to become an incarnation of the Goddess? How would your life and witness compare to that of the "goddesses" of olden times, such as Jezebel, Herodias, Salome, and others? Would you, for example, identify with this angry statement by a prominent New Ager:

> For the intellectual benefit of the biblical Fundamentalist, yes, the world is a lot more liberal than it used to be, but we believe it is that way not because the devil made it that way, but because *we* made it that, because we like that way. We like other kinds of music than hymns; we liked jazz in the 20s and 30s, and now we like rock. We also like 'suggestive' dancing, and movies, and drinking, and some of us even take drugs. And yes, we are trying to enjoy sex for recreational purposes rather than just procreational. Admittedly, some of us still feel a lot of guilt in this area, but . . . a lot of our guilts hopefully may be laid to rest.[8]

This revealing statement by the author of *From Eden to Eros: Origins of the Put Down of Women* has no doubt been echoed by tens of thousands of women. Perhaps you have heard similar comments from those who reject the tenets of Christianity and refuse the God of the Bible in their lives. For them, the New Age seems to be a way to escape the judgment that is to come. They desperately yearn to be free from guilt and shame. Instead of accepting the liberty that is in Christ our Lord, they are quick to embrace a religion which enticingly and lyingly whispers in their ear: "erase all guilt, accept no shame, there is no such thing as sin, you are your own God, a Goddess, you are the judge, there is no judgment, do as *you* will. There is no external guide. Seek the Goddess within. Invite her, your higher self, to rule. Don't worry, be happy."

The women of the New Age insist that salvation can come other than through Jesus Christ. And certainly, they reject the concepts of sin and redemption through Jesus Christ:

> And now, for the spiritual benefit of the biblical Fundamentalist, let me say that none of the above 'licentiousness' of today has anything whatsoever to do with our salvation. Some of us try drinking to get to God, and others thought they could find him through drugs, and still others tried sex to find the Goddess, but whatever our separate paths, we reject utterly your contention that our salvation may be possible through your squabbling churches, and only by following your Commandments and dogma.[9]

It is very sad to read the above. The author's frustration and bitterness clearly show through. It is indicative of Satan's success that so many women are searching hungrily for spirituality and truth in all the wrong places--ever seeking and never fulfilled. They turn to and fro, moving from sexual promiscuity to drinking, from tranquilizers to TV soap opera fantasizing. Some seek solace as career women; others fill up their empty

204   NEW AGE LIES TO WOMEN

lives in shopping forays or by volunteering for community and other activities. Still unfulfilled, they cry out in anger against God and His people.

"Why am I so unhappy? I've got it all," the liberated Aquarian woman complains. The answer is, of course, available. They *don't* have it all. Human beings cannot remain happy for long without Jesus Christ. We're just not built that way. As long as a woman chooses to serve the Goddess and the Adversary over Christ, she will remain in a state of emotional unrest and semi-misery, bound up in spiritual chains. That, regrettably, is the destiny of the liberated Aquarian woman.

THIRTEEN

The Lifestyle of the Liberated Aquarian Woman

If we say that we have no sin, we deceive ourselves, and the truth is not in us. If we confess our sins, He is faithful and just to forgive us our sins, and to cleanse us from all unrighteousness. If we say that we have not sinned, we make Him a liar, and His Word is not in us.

(I John 1:8-10)

Quit blaming ourselves . . . put the screws to guilt. Shame and guilt serve no long term purpose. . . . Stop the "shoulds" . . . we need to forgive ourselves. . . . If people tell us, directly or indirectly, that we ought to be ashamed, we don't have to believe it. . . . We need to value ourselves . . . and enhance our self-esteem.

Melodie Beattie
Co-dependent No More

T he New Age is upon us," exults Alice Bailey, "that which is old and undesirable must go." One of the things that the New Age wants to see go is the joyous, wholesome, and god-fearing lifestyle of the Christian woman and mother.

206 NEW AGE LIES TO WOMEN

Women are to exchange this lifestyle for one more liberated and open, one more broad and accepting of the new culture.

Guidance as to the lifestyle of the Goddess followers of today is found in the book *Secrets: A Practical Guide to Undreamed of Possibilities.* Written by Christina Thomas, this book is touted as a guide "for every adult who is ready to awaken their innate, sleeping potential." Thomas, who bills herself as a metaphysical teacher, a teacher of nero-linguistic programming, and a member of Self-Realization Fellowship, a New Age religious group, asserts that, "self condemnation is a direct violation of the Holy Spirit within each of us. One has no right to condemn himself."[1]

Thomas and other New Age authorities want women to believe that sin and guilt are outmoded Christian concepts. Belief in these antiquated ideas, New Agers urge, only serves to damage a person's self-esteem.

Obviously this is far different than what the Bible tells us. That in each person there is a witness to the truth of Jesus Christ and that in-built in every woman and man is a conscience, a guide, to moral behavior, and an understanding of those human paths which lead to happiness and those which can only lead to misery and pain.

The modern New Age psychologist tells you to believe that you must love yourself, warts and all. It doesn't matter what your decadent lifestyle might be--accept it, embrace it and boldly go forth into the New Age as a liberated woman. Thomas goes along with this unholy psychological mish-mash:

> Loving yourself includes accepting without judgement all your feelings . . . anger and guilt. It includes accepting both your emotions and the feelings in your body . . . you will then begin feeling the beautiful, loving, happy feelings.[2]

Nineteenth century New Age psychiatrist Carl Jung, explained this as the process of a woman's or man's embracing or owning their own *shadow*. Many New Agers today recommend that women get to know the *dragon* that lives within. They say, "sink into the darkness within, befriend the dragon." This, they contend, will allow you to mature and reach a higher level of consciousness and perfection. Is will enable you to become an Aquarian liberated woman:

> The whole purpose of repeated life times on earth is finally to remember your true identity as a perfect child of God. To the extent that in your mountain there is a solid rock of rigid false beliefs that you have not drilled into and dislodged, to the extent that there are monsters of fear slithering in the dark shadows of hidden caves, to that extent you have forgotten who you are. When you are ready, you will bore through the granite and head toward those monsters, as soon as you face them the caves become illuminated and you will see that this haunted house, so scary in the darkness, was just illusion all along.

> In Jungian terms, this process of facing the monsters within would be called 'owning your own shadow,' the shadow being all those qualities you have chosen to disown and subsequently, to make wrong and judge.[3]

How to Own Your Own Shadow and Reject Fundamentalism

The New Age counselors and therapists who are into Jungian psychology detest Christian fundamentalism. In effect, they despise the wisdom of God's Word. As one reads New Age literature, much of it written by modern psychologists and psychiatrists, constantly we come across references to persons who supposedly were damaged in childhood by fundamentalist Christian parents. This damage came, we are told, when the parents "forced" the children to go to Sunday school, to attend Bible studies, and when children were told that the United States is the greatest country in the world or that Jesus is the only way to salvation.

Also, it is considered very damaging and harmful to the "child within," according to the psychologists, to say "no," to insist that there are some things that are immoral, wrong or harmful to the child's development. In the New Age view, this is taking away from the freedom of the child so that he or she cannot grow up to become a full and mature New Age person. So goes the lie.

The psychologists also claim that we are damaged by "negative" thought processes which convince the individual that there is a judgment to come and a hell where bad, unsaved people go. The modern Goddess-woman rejects these ideas. Christina Thomas reports how one "skilled New Age facilitator" was able to "assist" a woman who was bound up by all of these feelings of guilt and sinfulness that had been "implanted" into her mind, obviously by fundamentalist parents. Here is the dialogue of the session between the facilitator and the woman as she was led through visualization and inner healing to reject the "negative" fundamentalist Christian values she learned from her parents:

Where are you?
In the womb.
What are you feeling?
I'm terrified.
Of what?
The devil is in here with me.
Where is he?
Behind me, turn around and look . . .

What do you see?
Nothing
Then what is it?
It's a thought . . . it's a belief!
Yeah, who's thought is it?
It's their belief, my parents, my father
Okay . . . and who else?
Me! It's my belief, I took on this belief.
That's right, it's your belief now. You have been
    carrying this thought around . . . that's why you've
    always been so careful to be such a good girl--you were
    afraid of this thought.
So now what can I do?[4]

It's apparent what the New Age answer to the pleas of this person was. Obviously, she was advised to embrace the devil by treating him as if he does not exist, that he's simply an illusion she invented and can now disinvent.

Once the person rejects all of the careful Christian training which was instilled in her as a child, then finally, she has become an acceptable candidate for incarnation by the Goddess. This is why this woman, after her session of visualization and rebirthing, and inner healing was heard to exclaim, "I felt my consciousness tremendously expanded. . .I felt total unconditional love for everyone and everything."[5]

Let Go of Your Guilt . . . Do as Thou Wilt

It is an undeniable fact that the New Age encourages women to let go of their guilt feelings and to reject the Christian teaching instilled in them from their childhood. No wonder the New Age has such magnetic appeal to women. It promises that you and I can do whatever we want, that we need not accept traditional Christian values and ethics but can, in a word, live like the devil and not suffer the consequences. Moreover, the New Age would have us believe that in rejecting guilt and simply admitting that we are lusty, unrepentant creatures, we can be healed.

What a marvelously wicked religion. Adultery, lies, anger, insane jealousy, fraud, greediness--it doesn't matter what our behavior, we simply exclaim, "well that's the way I am. I am what I am," and go about the devil's business. Worse, the New Age would have us believe that by accepting these pathetically low standards of womanhood we can be made *whole*. Not only that, but that we can experience love of ourselves and others. Certainly it is easy to love ourself or someone else if we have no standards, for then there is no measuring stick to judge whether our love is meaningful or has relevance. But this is a false love, a sick love. In truth, it is not love at all.

In effect, to be incarnated as the Goddess means to feel just fine and dandy about all the wrongs you commit and all the sins in your life. For example, in our files we have case reports of women who aborted children and later felt terribly sad and riddled with guilt. To resolve their guilt feelings, they did not turn to God and seek repentance but instead went to a New Age practitioner. Invariably the New Age teacher would take the person through some type of consciousness-changing exercise such as deep breathing, chanting, visualization, mental imagery, or inner healing. The end result is often a tragic denial of reality and a rejection of Biblically moral values.

For example, in one instance a young lady was told to visualize herself in a tunnel-like place moving toward a great light. She was to imagine that it was very warm and cozy there and full of love and then suddenly to realize that she was in a womb. There, in the womb, she was to recognize her child that had been aborted. Then, looking the child square in the face she was told to picture the infant telling her, "I forgive you, it's okay."

The young lady walked away from the New Age doctor's office relieved. "This wasn't bad after all," she said, "I feel so clean inside, I got it all out of my system. My consciousness has expanded so much my head feels like it will burst. I am light, pure light."⁶

What we have seen here though, was not light at all but darkness. We cannot absolve our guilt and our sin simply by proceeding through some imaginary process into a tunnel and envisioning forgiveness in this manner. God never intended for woman to suffer from guilt indefinitely, but he did give us a conscience so that *when* we sin, we feel guilty and we realize we need forgiveness. Moreover, the Bible gives us the good news that God, our redeemer, will forgive us if we simply go to him with our griefs, our sorrows, and our regretfulness. If we are truly repentant, he will receive us and wash us thoroughly from all unrighteousness. The overpowering stains and burdens we carry will be taken off our backs if we but call on Him and sincerely seek His love and forgiveness.

We can only conclude then, that the young lady who felt free of the guilt of aborting her baby was simply the victim of a satanic delusion. How true it is that the Bible tells us that in the last days many will be given over to a reprobate mind. I believe this young lady was a victim. A victim of the satanic New Age lie that we can be our own mediator, that we can work things out without the Most High God. Unfortunately, there are millions of young women, just like this one, who are convinced that it doesn't matter what their conduct is. They have been lied to and told that as long as they have the right *positive attitude*, they can be happy and fulfilled. Deep inside they know different.

Can the Goddess Religion Bring Happiness?

Most women today lead lives of quiet desperation. Misery is rampant in New Age America. The reason for this misery is that few today are living in the will of God. The Mother Goddess reigns supreme inside the breast of most women. The same was true of women in ancient times. Pagan women, too, were told that sin and guilt were of no significance. For example, in the Greek city of Sparta, historians say that women had total sexual freedom. Adultery was common and marriage was not taken very seriously. In fact, Plutarch reported that in Sparta the infidelity of women was even somewhat glorified. One historian, Nicholas of Damascus, tells us that a Spartan woman was entitled by society to have herself made pregnant by the handsomest man she could find.[7] All of this was in keeping with the decadent moral values of the Goddess Religion. Yet, all this "freedom" did not confer joy and happiness to women's lives.

Neither will today's feminist and women's rights movements bring lasting joy. Women in Babylon were granted women's rights. The same type of rights being demanded by women today. For example, a young bride continued to hold title to her own possessions. She could acquire property in her own name, take legal action, be a party to contracts and share in her husband's inheritance. Women could also request divorce.

Just north of Babylon, in the area known as Anatolia, present day Turkey, sometimes known as Asia Minor, the Great Goddess religion enabled women to rule over the men. Wrote one historian, "From of old they have been ruled by the women." In Anatolia they worshiped a female deity, known as Arinna, the Sun Goddess. Arinna supposedly had a god-husband who was symbolized as a storm god, or as lightning.[8] You'll recall in the Gospel of Luke that Jesus stated "I beheld Lucifer as lightning fall from heaven."

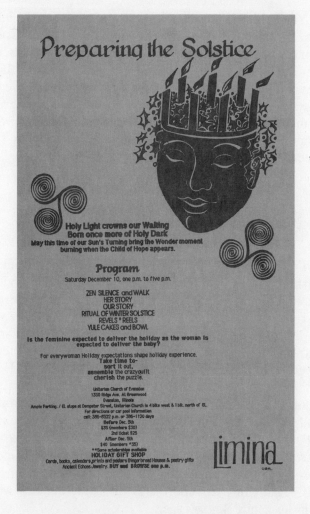

A women's group named "Limina" sponsored this gala at a Unitarian church in Evanston, Illinois. Again we see the pagan, candle-lit headdress of the Goddess.

Wording on this flyer reads in part: "Holy Light crowns our Waiting. Born once more of Holy Dark. May this time of our Sun's Turning bring the Wonder moment burning when the Child of Hope appears." The "Child" of the nature goddess, as we have seen, is none other than the coming "Son of perdition" (II Thessalonians 2).

You'll recall, too, that the city of Ephesus in biblical days contained the renowned temple of the Goddess Diana, sometimes called Artemis. Classical reports claim that this temple was founded by Amazon-like, that is, strong-willed women warriors.[9] Yet, when Paul preached Jesus in Ephesus many women were no doubt relieved to learn there was a real loving God who could forgive and accept them as his blessed children rather than as sexual objects and slaves of the flesh.

Rejection of God Results in Rebellion

In the Bible we find that the women of Israel who worshipped the Goddess were haughty and rebellious. When Jeremiah denounced them in the name of Almighty God, they answered him angrily declaring that they would not listen to his word that he had spoken in the name of Jehovah, but instead would go on doing all that they had vowed to do, offering incense to the Queen of Heaven and pouring libations--that is alcoholic drinks--in her honor. It is recorded in Jeremiah 44 that the women would go to the temple during the day while their men worked. The women would conduct ceremonies and worship the Queen of Heaven, the Mother Goddess. They would bake cakes for her with her features on them. It is a sad thing to report also that they did this without their husbands' knowledge.

How many of us know women today who are into false teachings and occultic practices without their husbands' knowledge? We often hear in Living Truth Ministries of such cases. For example, recently we were given the sad story of a thirty-four-year-old woman who began to communicate with a prisoner on death row because she "felt sorry for him." This prisoner had murdered three people in cold blood.   Through a series of letters, the woman convinced herself that "God" wanted her to continue to encourage this man.   Soon she was sending him money and even traveling a great distance to the prison to see him in person when visitation rules allowed.

When her husband found out about this he asked her not to go again.   He knew that this particular prisoner was a con artist who merely used gullible women.   But by this time she seemed to have a crush, or romantic fantasy, about this prisoner.   She defiantly told her husband that "God" wanted her to keep seeing the man.

The last we heard, she continued to periodically meet secretly with the prisoner and to send him money and gifts, all without her husband's knowledge.

In truth, this woman simply showed an utter lack of respect for her husband as well as a great degree of spiritual immaturity.   Can it not be said that she had taken on a form of Goddess consciousness in her rebellious activities and worldly desires?   The end result of such lack of submission and disobedience can be tragic.

In Israel, the end result of the women contemptuously going after the Goddess Astarte resulted in catastrophe for the entire nation.   Babylon invaded Jerusalem and its environs just as Jeremiah had prophesied and carried the people into captivity where they stayed for seventy years. Likewise, women who today invite the New Age Goddess to enter their lives are also brought into captivity-- spiritually and physically.   Regrettably, the period of their captivity may well last much, much longer than seventy years.   It could well last for an eternity.

We also find in the Old Testament reference to the reign of King Ahab and his Queen, Jezebel.   Jezebel, the daughter of the King of Sidon, evidently served as high priestess to Ashtoreth and Baal, the Mother Goddess and Father God of the pagans. Jezebel was a New Ager of her day.   You'll recall her wicked part in the seizing of Naboth's vineyard.   She was reportedly a woman who dressed fancily, decked with jewels and wearing expensive cosmetics. She enjoyed all of the regalia of her monarch position, yet, because she advocated idolatry and promoted the Goddess religion of immorality, her name has over the centuries become an infamous epithet for harlotry and rebelliousness. Again, the Bible makes us a witness to the tragic end result of Jezebel's defiance of God and her embracing of false gods and the goddess. Because of her treachery, Elijah prophesied this Word from the Lord, "The dogs shall eat Jezebel by the wall of Jezreel" (I Kings 22:23).

History records that this is exactly what happened to Jezebel. She was thrown off the wall of Jezreel and the dogs licked her blood. Likewise, her husband fell in battle, and the dogs licked his blood.

To become incarnated as the Goddess is to become a modern-day Jezebel. Now I know that, today, to call a woman a "Jezebel" is, basically, to call her a trollop and a tramp. But there are many women today--you and I know some--who lead respectable lives. No one would accuse them of being a Jezebel. Yet, their heart is as black as coal. And the reason why is clear. Unwittingly they have bought into the Goddess New Age religion by living the Goddess lifestyle.

The Co-dependency Excuse for Refusing Blame

A woman who becomes a Goddess, often without truly knowing she has been possessed by the spirit of evil, refuses blame and responsibility. The perfect example of this are those women who are into something called *co-dependency* counseling and treatment. The co-dependency movement has recently accelerated with the bestselling book by Melody Beattie *Co-dependent No*

More. Alcoholics Anonymous, the Adult Children of Alcoholics, and other twelve-step groups would have us believe that 99.9 percent of all women are victimized by the mysterious malady they call "co-dependency." In reality, co-dependency is extremely rare and certainly is nowhere near the problem that it's made out to be.

The co-dependency myth is that someone else is responsible for all our problems or for our unhappiness-- for example, parents, husband, children, the church, our employer, etc.

Beattie claims that co-dependency is caused when we don't feel good about ourselves. She states:

> Quit blaming ourselves . . . put the screws to guilt. Shame and guilt serve no long term purpose. . . . Guilt and shame are not useful as a way of life. Stop the 'shoulds' . . . we need to for give ourselves. . . . If people tell us, directly or indirectly, that we ought to be ashamed, we don't have to believe it . . . we need to value ourselves . . . and enhance our self esteem.[10]

Beattie's advice to women is similar to what we so often hear in the New Age counseling marketplace. She also suggests:

> Surrender to desire and gain energy, enthusiasm, mental zip, and even better health.[11]

The truth, however, is just the opposite. It depends on the object of your desire. An unholy desire can result in a *loss* of vital energy, a *dampening* of enthusiasm, a lamentable *lack* of mental zip and ultimately a *complete wrecking* of ones' physical and mental, not to mention spiritual, health.

The object of desire in the Goddess religion is *power*. *Self-empowerment* is one of the hottest phrases heard today from psychologists, religionists, and New Age teachers. This, too, is a concept emphasized by Melody Beattie and others in the co-dependency movement. Beattie approvingly quotes David Schwartz who in his bestseller, *The Magic of Thinking Big*, states, "Desire, when harnessed, is power."[12]

Isn't it enlightening and refreshing to recall that Jesus told us to deny ourselves and follow Him, to cast our cares and burdens on Him because He cares. Jesus told us that the meek--not the powerful--would inherit the earth.

From Bottle to Bondage

Another step toward union with the Goddess is to indulge in alcohol, narcotic, and other mind-altering drugs, and to abuse tranquilizers. Women are definitely the greatest abusers of tranquilizers today. And the number of women who have horrendous alcoholic problems and are hooked on cocaine, crack, and marijuana simply staggers the imagination.

This, too, is a carryover from the Babylonian Goddess religion. The demons of yesteryear in Babylon are still around today, encouraging women to calm their nerves with tranquilizers or to enhance their fun with alcohol. Alcohol, drugs taken to induce various mental states, and love potions were very common in Babylon, as they also were in Rome and Greece, where the Goddess was worshiped.

In his scholarly work, *Greek Religion*, Walter Burkert wrote of the drinking of wine and alcohol and the use of stimulants in the celebrations of the god Dionysos.[13] These were used in the Mystery ceremonies and orgies to create a sense of sexual excitement and to liberate the inhibitions of men and women. How much is this like today! So many people drink socially claiming that it lubricates communications. They say they drink to make themselves feel better so that they can be more free and loose. Again we see the cycle. The desires of the mind which were stimulated by the Goddess of ancient days are similarly stimulated today in twentieth century America.

Not By One Avenue Alone

There are many pathways to Satan: drug and alcohol abuse, sexual perversions and indiscretions, incitement of anger and jealousy; disobedience; an uncooperative spirit; participation in occult activities. All of these things and more are signs that a woman has given in to the Goddess. And this is exactly what Satan desires. It is evidence that a woman is slowly but surely metamorphosing into the very image of the Goddess. Satan has so many avenues through which he leads women blinded by the light.

Interestingly enough, Margot Adler, a prominent pagan, occultist, and New Age witch, in her bestselling book, *Drawing Down the Moon*, discusses exactly this. She writes that the real message of drawing down the moon is that *diversity* alone can save us. Adler believes that the spiritual realm of a woman craves and deserves diversity. "Only by an extraordinary abundance of disparate spiritual paths," she says, "will human beings navigate a pathway through the dark and swirling storms that mark our current era. Not by one avenue alone can we arrive at so tremendous a secret."[14]

Adler is correct in the sense that Satan offers so many alternatives, so many options. Not by one avenue alone does a person arrive at so tremendous and so horrible a secret. *That secret, so terrible and frightening, is this: Satan wants you to be molded into the image of the Goddess.*

Are You Being Transformed into the Spirit of the Goddess?

Consider this: you may deny that you are a New Age believer. You may say, "I don't believe in crystals, I've never been to a spirit channeling session, I don't like the smell of incense, I don't believe in the ungodly doctrines of reincarnation and karma, I'm okay." But regardless of whether or not you've swallowed the pill of the New Age in all its utter depravity, you may nevertheless at this very moment be in dire danger of being possessed by the spirit of the Goddess.

Each time you commit adultery, in deed or in thought; each time you watch soap operas and other television shows that so flagrantly defy good morals and biblical standards; each time you read a fantasy novel which causes sexual lust to be stirred; each time you drink liquor, smoke, curse, lie, abuse tranquilizers, or read occult books; each time you attend twelve-step programs where Jesus Christ is not honored and most in attendance believe in a *god of their own choosing* or in a *higher power* other than Jesus; each time you fail to read God's Word and express your love toward Him, *you are being transformed into the image of the Goddess.*

We are told in the Bible, "be not transformed to this world but be ye transformed by the renewing of your mind" (Romans 12:2). However, just the opposite is happening with the majority of women. They are transforming themselves to the world whose god, temporarily, is Lucifer. The Goddess is incarnated in their very souls. *She* is alive. But *they* are dead.

FOURTEEN

Back to the Future

There shall not be found among you any one that maketh his son or his daughter to pass through the fire, or that useth divination . . . or an enchanter, or a witch. . . . For all that do these things are an abomination unto the Lord.

(Deuteronomy 18:10, 12)

This was the hottest fire I had seen. . . . the firewalking exercise took my breath away. People began to move more swiftly to the coals . . . (My six-year-old) Teo suddenly grasped my hand and pulled me to the fire. . . . About two-thirds of the way across, he whimpered, Mom, it's getting hot.

Chris Griscom
Ecstasy is a New Frequency

In Chapter One we looked at the growing evidence that the New Age has revived the practices of Mystery Babylon. Now in this chapter, we will peer even deeper into the black goings-on of today's New Age religion. These true, documented cases are proof positive that the Goddess is, indeed back . . . with a vengeance.

Enlightenment is a Cosmic Sexual Experience

If the sun and stars are living beings and the universe is, as a whole, a living body, can we humans have intimate physical relations with these planetary bodies? Or is what Chris Griscom reveals below a case of sexual relations with a demon spirit? Or is there another explanation?

It was an odyssey we had made before . . . going down to the gentle desert around Tucson at Christmas. I felt whole and happy--sleeping, eating, exploring together in an environment without superficial distraction.

It seemed perfect to sleep out under the stars on Christmas Eve. The beauty, the newness, the vulnerability of it sparked by unquenchable emotion which soared up into the night sky. The expansion stirred my body. . . . It had been four months since I had made love and I mused about the serious possibility that I would never experience those sensations again. I was forty-one, my sexual energy honed to its sweetest, highest pitch. I laughed to myself at the thought that what I had experienced in the last several years made me feel bursting, as if I alone had made a new discovery which would change the world. Here I was, fresh with this new "stuff," and now I was never to revisit its secret world.

I don't know how long I slept, but I awakened to a trillion orgasmic explosions, pulsating electrical spasms shattering the confines of my cells, my body, my consciousness!

I was streaming. All borders, all awareness of where I began and ended was gone. After indescribable, timeless moments, it quieted into a sensation of an undulating sea and I realized that I had literally levitated more than a foot above the ground. I felt a sensation of floating down, and for the rest of the night I listened to a wonderful humming within my body. My cells were singing. My mind never stirred itself throughout, I was so engulfed in the experience. Only now could I give it a name: I call it "cosmic orgasm."[1]

Initiation by Fire

The Bible expressly forbids firewalking and other pagan fire rituals (see Deuteronomy 18). But this is a hot trend today in the New Age, as the account below reveals.

It was to be our first graduation ceremony at The Light Institute. . . . I have always known that some day we would perform miracles ourselves, just as it has been foretold.

With a twinkle in my eye, I proposed a firewalk. Firewalks are a perfect example of bringing into experiential reality the "impossibles" of our limited minds. I was delighted as my colleagues-to-be accepted the "initiation by fire."

Appropriately, I had already put myself through this kind of initiation and had walked a thrilling nineteen times before. To push the edge for myself, I vowed to be the first one across the fire.

It was a group of about 45, which included three of my children: Karin, who was being initiated as a colleague; Megan, age thirteen; and Teo, age six. This was the hottest fire I had seen. The flames reached about fifteen feet and the person tending was standing far back from it. It took three hours for those flames to die down enough to create the bed of coals, which stretched out more than sixteen feet.

We stood in a ring of clasped hands around the coals,
which were by now glowing a beautiful yellow-white color.
Though I knew by their color that they were at their
hottest temperature, they seemed gentle and soothing to
me, almost mesmerizing. I felt as if we were made of the
same stuff. I broke the circle and stepped up onto the bed.
Across my face I felt the dancing flicker of a burning log,
which had not yet relinquished itself to coal. Fixing my
sight on a spot at the other end, I began to pull myself
towards it. I felt like a wind gently lifting and falling as I
moved along. . . . After a timeless moment, I stepped off
onto the other side.

Exhilaration and ecstatic joy swept through my being. I
had to fight my body to keep from jumping into the air--
but it was someone else's turn. To my surprise, Megan
stepped to the edge. I remember how my breath and heart
became stilled. I watched her young grace as she glided
across with a sureness that brought tears to my eyes. She
circled around to stand next to me and in a very strong,
knowing voice said, "Mom, I'll never have to die of cancer.
Maybe I'll never die at all!"

People began to move more swiftly to the coals and I felt
an exhilarated energy-pattern begin to form itself. Teo
suddenly grasped my hand and pulled me to the fire. We
stepped up together and began our walk. About two-thirds
of the way across, she whimpered, "Mom, it's getting hot."
I answered, "You can do it, Teo, you can, you can," and we
reached the end and jumped into the pool of water
awaiting us. It was too much for me; I was so elated, I let
out a little yell. Everyone was experiencing the same
exuberance, and people began to join each other in twos
and walk across the fire.

We all shared such a feeling of empowerment. We were
truly a group of "untouchables". . . . It was a feeling of
belonging to something good and joyous: a force of light.[2]

"The Planet is Healed"

A demon disguised as the Mother Goddess is appearing to many New Agers. The account here comes from John Randolph Price, head of the Planetary Commission.

> In February 1985, during a group rebirthing session in the mountains of northern Georgia, I was taken back to just before this incarnation--then carried into the future where I experienced the most beautiful vision of my entire life. There seemed to be millions (billions?) of us, all moving up the side of a mountain, each carrying a lighted candle in our right hand. There was no effort in climbing the mountain . . . it was as though we were on level ground, yet there was the sensation of moving up. At one point I looked up and back--and as far as I could see in both directions were men, women and children, and the fire from those individual candles seemed to illumine the world with dazzling light. As we all reached the top, a beautiful *Light Being in the form of a woman* raised her arms and spoke these words: "The planet is healed."
>
> I simply cannot describe the emotion that I felt at that moment.[3]

A Feminist Ritual for the Goddess

The following outline for a feminist ritual is one of a number produced by a workshop of around thirty-five women from all over the United States.

GREETING
(The gathered group exchanges words and signs of peace)

INVOKING THE POWER OF THE GODDESS

PRAYER OF CONFESSION
(A unison prayer expressing ways we participate in our own
 oppression by not claiming the power of being)

Then, the poem "For the Unknown Goddess", by Elizabeth
Brewster, is read:

> Lady, the unknown goddess,
> we have prayed long enough only
> To Yahweh the thunder god.
>
> Now we should pray to you again
> goddess of a thousand names and faces
> Ceres Venus Demeter Isis
> Ianna Queen of Heaven
> or by whatever name
> you would be known
>
> You who sprang from the sea
> you who are present in the moisture of love
> who live in the humming cells
> of all life. . .
> and you who are earth
> you with your beautiful ruined face
> wrinkled by all
> that your children have done to you. . .
>
> we invoke your name
> which we no longer know
>
> and pray to you
> to restore our humanity
> as we restore your divinity.

The order of service now continues:

A RITUAL RESPONSE
(Lying on the floor to listen to the humming in our cells; a
 walk outside to become aware of the earth; a meditation,
 repeating phrases, noting emotions evoked by the poem,
 etc.)

SILENCE
PRAYERS
BLESSING RITUAL
(The women turn to one another and ask for words and
  signs of blessing. This may be done individually or
  collectively, such as in the laying on of hands.)

THE END[4]

Signs of the New Age: The Goddess on Television

The full moon is seen in the centre of the television screen.
Clouds are moving slowly across it. A vague impression of
awe is established by the sound of women's voices
chanting. The chanting induces a sense of indefinable
unease. The camera moves to an altar of some kind.
Between purple candles stands a female image. Suddenly,
a calm and authoritative female narrator explains:

> It is the night of the full moon--a special time for
> women according to folk-lore. These women are
> worshipping their God, Inanna. Inanna is a female
> God.

The camera now shows a veiled priestess, leading the ritual
for a small group of women in a suburban house in the
north of England. The voice continues:

> Rediscovering the Goddess tradition is one of the
> ways in which women are beginning to question the
> generally accepted view that God is Male.

The program title appears on the screen: GOD THE
MOTHER. Now, the priestess is shown explaining her
religion, still "veiled before strangers":

It is the mother who generates all things out of
herself; it is the mother who nourishes, who gives milk;
she is the primordial being, so to speak. . . if any
human being is in God's image, it is the mother who,
before any other, is in God's image. It is to the mother
that we turn from the beginning of life and it is really
in the mother that we see God.[5]

The Devil's Language: New Age Speaking in Tongues

I heard a babble of voices in strange languages. I didn't
know what I was supposed to do with them, but I knew that
something was expected of me. Suddenly I began to chant
words in a loud, ringing voice: 'Sumari, Ispania, Wena
nefarie, Dena dena nefarie, Lona, Lona, Lona Sumare.'
Then in a whisper someone else said in my voice, in other
words coming from my mouth, but it was someone from
inside of me, 'I am Sumari, you are Sumari, throughout the
ages you have been Sumari. I am acquainting you with
your heritage.' At the same time a delicious warmth filled
my body. It came like a glow, from inside, radiating
outward.[6]

This was how psychologist Jane Roberts described her
first experience in speaking in tongues. Now keep in mind
this was not Christian speaking in tongues but a New Age
unholy counterfeit of the Christian tongues experience.

The late Jane Roberts wrote a number of books which
she said were channeled through her by her spirit guide
Seth. Today these books are tremendous bestsellers in B.
Dalton, Waldenbooks, and other book stores throughout
the United States and even around the world. There is
also a Seth International organization headquartered in
Austin, Texas. Each year Seth International conducts an
annual Seth World Conference in which intensive
seminars, workshops, and training are held.

In common with other spirit guides (demons), Seth told his human counterpart, Jane Roberts, that women are their own gods. That bisexuality and lesbianism are perfectly fine lifestyles, that there is no right or wrong--man makes his own rules, and that the Bible is no more an inspired set of scriptures than any other "holy books."

Once Roberts opened herself up to this demonic entity, then she also was taught how to speak in tongues. Based on her experiences Roberts wrote:

> The Sumari (tongues) language is not a language in the ordinary sense. It's importance lies in its sounds, not its written patterns. The sounds to things. The meaning is apart from the power of the sounds, and rides on as fish swim in water.

Seth International encourages its followers and students to speak and sing in tongues. In fact, in 1988 Seth conducted seminars led by Toni Kosydar, a former high school teacher and coach from Reno, Nevada, who led students in speaking and singing this other-worldly language. As befits a counterfeit, Kosydar insists that the New Age speaking in tongues, as practiced by Seth, is a "gift."

Seth is not the only New Age group that practices speaking in tongues. Missionaries to India report that many of the gurus and the disciples in their ashrams speak in tongues. Meanwhile, many Americans who are involved in spirit channelings and spiritualism are today being taught how to speak in tongues.

The Hindu guru, Bhagwan Shree Rajneesh, whose American commune in Oregon came into some disrepute a few years back, has been known to speak in tongues frequently as do his many admirers and disciples. In the *New York Times* recently, reporter Jane Cross visited a United States center of the Bhagwan in Seattle, Washington. She reported that the place was very busy with "lots of hand-shaking and speaking in tongues." Rajneesh supporters at the center, said Gross, also came regularly for sessions on laughing and had also spent an entire week crying, plus another week meditating.[7]

The Bhagwan himself, deported from the United States, now carries on a nightly discourse at his ashram (worship center) in Poona, India. His disciples blame themselves for his deportation. "It was our own fault as he now tells us," said one Mr. Majida. "We didn't take responsibility ourselves. Now we will be more alert." Another disciple quoted by reporter Jane Cross, Mashanti Gopura, an American woman who had changed her name, stated, "the growth I experienced is unbelievable. This is not an ordinary guy," she said referring to Rajneesh, "you don't judge him by ordinary standards. When you lay your neck down for the Bhagwan you're saying, yes master, take my head."[8]

That Satan would counterfeit things of God should not at all surprise Christians. The Bible clearly tells us to try the spirits so we can judge whether or not they come from God.

Of Wizards and Sorcerers: Arthur, Taliesin and Merlin

A burgeoning, fast growth subject area for kids' and adult books is that of wizards and sorcerers. Occultic New Age books about the sorcery of the Druid and Celtic witchcraft sect in ancient England are proliferating. Three such books--which claim to be "Christian" but, because of their characters, settings, and plot, are decidedly occultic in theme--are *Arthur*, *Merlin* and *Taliesin*, published by Crossway Books and written by Stephen Lawhead.

Taliesin, the High Priest of Satan's Druid Religion

Research into the true meaning of Taliesin shows him to be a legendary occult magical character who was initiated into the wicked Druidic witchcraft sect and became a High Priest.

Murray Hope, author and researcher of pagan religions, examines the Taliesin character thoroughly in the book *Practical Celtic Magic*. Taliesin, Hope points out, practiced witchcraft, claimed to be a reincarnated being who had lived many past lives, was once the Sun God, and worshiped the Mother Goddess, as did all Druids. Taliesin was also claimed to be Merlin the Magician, reincarnated.[9]

"That Taliesin represents a profound occult truth," writes Hope, "there is little doubt."[10]

Incredibly, in his book *Taliesin*, author Lawhead attempts to portray sorcerer Taliesin to Christians in a favorable, heroic and romantic light, even suggesting that he became "Christian." Perhaps Lawhead could explain to his readers why Taliesin is so prominently mentioned by Satanist Manley P. Hall in his classic 1928 book, *The Secret Teachings of All Ages*.[11] It would also be wise for would-be readers of *Taliesin* to consider that Lawhead's book is proclaimed on the front cover to be "the first book of the Pendragon Cycle." They would also be well-advised to consider the setting of this "Christian" novel: lost Atlantis, the much lauded kingdom of the New Age where the sun god Bel (or Baal) dominated. Note, too, that Lawhead is also author of an abomination called *The Dragon King Trilogy*.

In *Taliesin*, author Lawhead begins his saga with an occultic flair, writing:

I weep no more for the lost, asleep in their watery graves.
The voices of the departed speak: Tell our story, they say.
And so I take my pen and write.[12]

It is clear that Christians and secularists alike are being taken in by the book *Taliesin*. But the most mind-boggling thing imaginable is this fact: The Evangelical Christian Publishers Association, an industry group made up of America's largest Christian publishers, *selected Taliesin as "The Best Christian Novel of 1988," presenting the author with its Gold Medallion Award.*

The Awful Truth About the Celts and Druids

In Lawhead's *Taliesin*, the female heroine, Charis, comes to Celtic Britain from Atlantis where she was a ritual bull dancer. John Sharkey, in his well-researched guide, *Celtic Mysteries: The Ancient Religion*, reveals the occultic meaning of this, showing that the Celtic peoples first emigrated to Britain and Ireland from the Indus Valley in India. Therefore, he reports, religions and "cultural affinities between the Celts and India can be traced in the animal *rituals* in which the spirit of the new king or queen is rendered *incarnate* with that of a bull."[13] The Celts, notes Sharkey, "were at one with the elements of the Great Spirit." They "comingled local deities with others from Greek and Asian legends." The Goddess and the Sun God were their principal deities.

Alexander Hislop affirms this. He writes that the "worship of Bel (the Sun God) and Astarte (the Goddess) were very early introduced into Great Britain, along with the Druids.[14]

The Celts and Druids practiced gruesome rituals of human sacrifice. Sharkey describes one such ritual in which the victim is first "made drunk with mead and led into the middle of a circle of twelve stones arranged around an oak." He is tied to the oak where he is then cruelly "beaten, flayed, blinded or castrated, impaled upon a mistletoe stake and finally hacked into joints on the altar stone."[15]

"All this," records Sharkey, "is done with the utmost ceremony, and his blood, caught in a stone basin, is sprinkled over the whole tribe. All those present partake (eat) of the body of the dead . . . to make them vigorous and fruitful."[16]

Stephen Lawhead also attempts to portray *Arthur* and *Merlin*, two other pagan sorcery characters, in a favorable light, making them into romantic heroes whose exploits and spirituality, says Lawhead, aided the ushering of Christianity into early Britain. The truth is horrendously just the opposite. Sharkey writes that Arthur and Merlin are the most popular of the Sun God heroes.[17]

The Roman conquerors of Britain in 60 A.D. found the religious system perversely evil and breathtakingly grotesque. They discovered blood-stained groves of trees; howling, black-clad priests; screaming and violent women. Julius Caesar himself told of mass burnings by these pagans of human and animal victims in huge wicker cages.[18]

Merlin the Magician is honored today by the New Age and occult world as a sorcerer and shaman *par excellence*. As Page Bryant comments in his article in a New Age magazine, *Wildfire*, "One of the figures that stands out as the epitome of shamanism is Merlin . . . Merlin embodies the path of the shaman."[19]

Page Bryant also talks about the New Age revival of King Arthur, relating it to spirit channeling (in other words, demonic entities). Bryant reports that in a channeling from the spirit world given in Glastonbury, England in 1987, the Spirit Teacher "spoke, in-depth, of the re-awakening of Arthur the King."[20] It has also been reported that Merlin's spirit has been appearing to many occultists and spirit channelers, both in England and the U.S.[21]

234 NEW AGE LIES TO WOMEN

Lawhead, who no doubt would deny it, is in reality an accomplice to this demonic re-awakening of Arthur, as well as Merlin the Sorcerer, and Taliesin, the Druid Priest. What Lawhead is doing is merging this ancient evil with Christianity. It just won't do, being another gospel--an accursed gospel (Galatians 1).

FIFTEEN

The Beautiful Woman: Crystal Clear Answers to Dark New Age Lies

See, I have set before thee this day life and good, and death and evil. . . . Therefore, choose life.
(Deuteronomy 30:15, 19)

There is a way that seemeth right to a man; but the end thereof are the ways of death.
(Proverbs 14:12)

I can't believe they did those things to me," she cried, tears streaming down her cheeks. "They lied . . . Oh, Lord, they lied. How could I have been so blind, so deceived. . . . How?"

My heart went out to Diane. She certainly wasn't the first woman I had counseled whose heart was broken and whose life was in tatters because of the sinister deception of the New Age. But her situation was perhaps the most poignant and revealing.

For eighteen long years--since the age of 16--Diane had hungered and searched for Truth amid the haze and fog of New Age cults and religions. Rejecting the Christianity of her parents as "old-fashioned and ignorant," she had become a hippie of sorts, spouting peace slogans and embracing every mystical word and mantra of gurus and holy men whom she encountered in the bizarre New Age sub-culture. Some introduced her to drugs and alcohol, others to "holy sex," meditation, chanting and body deprivations. However, none of these so-called "enlightened masters" could provide the enduring answers or the satisfaction and happiness Diane desperately longed for.

In her quest, Diane traveled on a pilgrimage to India with her Hindu guru. She served within the bowels of the ship at sea operated by Scientology and became a priestess of a New Age Liberal Catholic Church. She feverishly volunteered as a worker for Unity churches, toiled as a peon inside the commune of a Lady Guru who claimed to have achieved "Goddess Consciousness," and served as the personal aide, secretary and sexual slave to a Native American Indian Chief. For a while he had her convinced that she was a reincarnated Cherokee Indian named "Singing Bird" in a previous life. She left this "Great Teacher" after his repeated physical beatings and mental abuse became too much for her to handle.

Still, Diane searched, each day bringing a false hope, then a let down in spirit when the radiant promises of a particular New Age teacher or program failed to materialize. Finally, at the end of her rope, in abject misery, one day Diane thought of killing herself, of ending it all. But suddenly, a thought--a glimmer of light beckoning from within--startled her. "Could Jesus," she asked herself, "really be the answer?" Could it be that my parents were right all along? Is He truly the way, the truth and the life? Diane fell to her knees and pleaded with God to forgive her for ever doubting Him. She asked

Jesus to save her and come into her, to make her whole, to heal her hurts and her brokenness.

And He did! Miraculously, in a way that only He Himself knows how, Jesus gave Diane a gift so incredible, so marvelously complete, that she could scarcely believe it. But she knew it was so. Inside her breast was the proof. Jesus knew her and she knew Him. Her inquiry had come to an end. The quest was over, but life for Diane had only begun.

Jesus Christ provided Diane with all the crystal clear answers she needed to dispel the dark lies of Satan's New Age movement and religion. What He provided was Himself.

Satan comes to women in a million disguises today, ever probing their weaknesses, hoping to move in and take control whenever he finds vulnerability. His New Age religion promises a smorgasbord of eternal delicacies, spiritual treats and favors. But it's not filling--just so many empty "calories." Worse, it's laced with poisons and toxins that kill and destroy and wreck and mutilate a woman's soul and spirit. In the end, there is only blackness and despair.

Jesus offers exactly the opposite. His is not a complicated way. His way is not a bewildering hodge-podge of never-ending doctrines and practices--ranging from crystals and UFO's to spirit channeling, Eastern mysticism, and barren meditation. His is not a religion, not a program or regimen of classes and instruction. Just *Him*. Jesus simply says to you and me, "Come unto me, all ye that are burdened and heavy-laden and I will give you rest." There is liberty in Christ Jesus. He came into our world, taking upon himself human flesh for a brief period, not to condemn women and men, but to save them.

Are You Searching?

Perhaps you, too, are searching. Possibly you have looked into a number of philosophies and ideas, read a variety of books and bibles about religion and spirituality, and talked with a number of friends and acquaintances regarding religion and the meaning of life. It could be that on your journey you have encountered many New Age teachings, even dabbled in the occult. Maybe you examined the confusing and unfulfilling doctrines of so-called "Christian" religions such as Mormonism and Jehovah's Witnesses.

If so, you are not alone. Tens of thousands--even millions of men and women--have trod the same path or paths. I know. In the past four years alone I have had the opportunity to talk with and witness to so many who are bewildered, mixed-up, or just plain miserable because they are unable to discern for themselves which religion to follow, or what "new revelation" or "inspiring" teacher to tune into.

So why condemn yourself to a lifetime of emptiness? Why seek after the falsehoods and lies of the New Age when the only True God, who loves you so much he suffered and died on the cross for your sins and mine, calls out to you, tenderly and earnestly pleading, "Come unto me . . . and I will give you rest."

The Two Alternatives

Jesus wishes no one to perish; He wants all to know and trust Him, to enter into a never-ending lifetime of joy, bright promise and contentment. But each of us chooses at whose side we will stand. On the one hand Satan offers to you his elusive New Age religion, Mystery Babylon, and his Goddess. On the other, there stands Jesus Christ--the Jesus of the Bible, the glorious King of all, with arms outstretched and with all-encompassing love in His tender eyes. No matter what your physical shape, size, or facial features, He loves you. You are made beautiful the moment you accept His love.

Judgment of Babylon and Her Children

If you choose Satan's way and reject Jesus, you should know the facts about what your decision ultimately will mean for your life. It's only fair and right that you know that God has already declared a sentence on those whom He, in His omniscience, knows will reject Him and instead follow the reckless and limited path of the Adversary. God has already passed judgment on Mystery Babylon and all those who defiantly enter into its spiritual gates. The Goddess, too--that unholy myth and creation of Satan, has been judged and her punishment decreed.

If you have indeed hardened your heart and will not pay heed to Jesus' pleas of salvation and redemption, then know what shall be the outcome.

God's judgment on Babylon, its lies and liars, is found in the pages of His Word, in Isaiah 47. Below is printed, without abridgement, his righteous decree:

1 Come down, and sit in the dust, O virgin daughter of Babylon, sit on the ground: there is no throne O daughter of the Chaldeans: for thou shalt no more be called tender and delicate.

2 Take the millstones, and grind meal: uncover thy locks, make bare the leg, uncover the thigh, pass over the rivers.

3 Thy nakedness shall be uncovered, yea, thy shame shall be seen: I will take vengeance, and I will not meet thee as a man.

4 As for our Redeemer, the Lord of hosts is his name, the Holy One of Israel.

5 Sit thou silent, and get thee into darkness, O daughter of the Chaldeans: for thou shalt no more be called, The lady of kingdoms.

6 I was wroth with my people, I have polluted mine inheritance, and given them into thine hand: thou didst show them no mercy; upon the ancient hast thou very heavily laid thy yoke.

7 And thou saidst, I shall be a lady for ever: so that thou didst not lay these things to thy heart, neither didst remember the latter end of it.

8 Therefore, hear now this, thou that art given to pleasures, that dwellest carelessly, that sayest in thine heart, I am, and none else besides me; I shall not sit as a widow, neither shall I know the loss of children:

9 But these two things shall come to thee in a moment in one day, the loss of children, and widowhood: they shall come upon thee in their perfection for the multitude of thy sorceries, and for the great abundance of thine enchantments.

10 For thou hath trusted in thy wickedness: thou hast said, None seeth me. Thy wisdom and thy knowledge, it hath perverted thee; and thou hast said in thine heart, I am, and none else besides me.

11 Therefore shall evil come upon thee; thou shalt not know from whence it riseth: and mischief shall fall upon thee; thou shalt not be able to put it off and desolation shall come upon thee suddenly, which thou shalt not know.

12 Stand now with thine enchantments, and with the multitude of thy sorceries, wherein thou hast laboured from thy youth; if so be thou shalt be able to profit, if so be thou mayest prevail.

13 Thou art wearied in the multitude of thy counsels. Let now the astrologers, the stargazers, the monthly prognosticators, stand up, and save thee from these things that shall come upon thee.

14 Behold, they shall be as stubble; the fire shall burn them; they shall not deliver themselves from the

power of the flame: there shall not be a coal to warm at, nor fire to sit before it.

15 Thus shall they be unto thee with whom thou hast laboured, even thy merchants, from thy youth: they shall wander every one to his quarter; none shall save thee.

Choose Life

God's judgments are always righteous and we can have confidence that His will shall prevail. The prophets in our Bible made many prophecies, and, amazingly each has come to pass, just as foretold. The destiny of Babylon and all who follow the Goddess is foreordained. Their final day, too, shall come and events transpire exactly as Isaiah prophesied.

If you do not know Jesus Christ as your Lord and Savior, I pray that you will release your burdens to Him today. Please . . . don't fall for Satan's *New Age Lies to Women*. Choose life!

> *See, I have set before thee this day life and good, and death and evil. . . . Therefore, choose life.*
> (Deuteronomy 30:15, 19)

Notes

CHAPTER 1: Satan's Mistress and Her New Age Lies to Women

1. Barbara Marx Hubbard, *The Hunger of Eve* (Eastsound, Washington: Island Pacific NW, 1989) pp. 8-9.
2. Rickie Moore, *A Goddess In My Shoes* (Atlanta, Georgia: Humanics New Age, 1988), pp. 75-90.
3. Miriam Starhawk, see "Witchcraft and the Religion of the Green Goddess," *Yoga Journal*, May-June 1986, also see *Circle Network News*, Circa 1987, and Texe Marrs, *Mystery Mark of the New Age* (Crossway Books, 1988), p. 204.
4. A pagan/goddess witchcraft ritual described by Naomi Goldenberg in *Changing of the Gods* (Boston, Massachusetts: Beacon Press, 1979) pp. 86-87.
5. From the book, *L. Ron Hubbard: Madman or Messiah?*, by Bert Corydon and L. Ron Hubbard, Jr. (Secaucus, New Jersey: Lyle Stuart, Inc., 1987) pp. 32-33.
6. From the introduction of *The Satanic Witch*, by Anton LaVey (Los Angeles, California: Feral House, 1989)
7. Dr. Robert Ulman, *The New Times*, Seattle,Washington, October 1988.

CHAPTER 2: From Hollywood to Capitol Hill

1. Jose Arguelles, interviewed in *Meditation* magazine, Summer 1987, Vol. II., No. 3, pp. 6-19. Also see Antero Alli, "A Post-Convergence Interview with Jose Arguelles, *Magical Blend* Magazine, Issue 18, 1988. Pp. 17-20.
2. Jose Arguelles, interviewed in *Whole Life Times*, Vol. #3, 1987, pp. 63-66, and see the references under footnote number 1 above.
3. Marilyn Ferguson, *The Aquarian Conspiracy: Personal and Social Transformation in the 1980's*, (Los Angeles, California: J. P. Tarcher, Inc., 1980)
4. John Randolph Price, *The Planetary Commission* (Austin, Texas: Quartus Books, 1984).
5. *Commission Update (Report)* Planetary Commission for Global Healing, Austin, Texas, March 1988, p. 4.
6. Ibid.
7. See Cliff Kincaid, "More Wisdom From Ted Turner," *Human Events*, August 2, 1986, p. 14; and Dave Price, "Broadcaster Ties Survival to 'New Age' President," *The Denver Post*, June 15, 1986, p. 2-B. Also, see *USA Today*, July 20, 1989; *Human Events*, August 12, 1989; and the *Better World Society* promotional brochure.

8. "The Twilight Zone in Washington," *U. S. News & World Report,* Dec. 5, 1988, pp. 24-30.

9. Ibid.

10. See Jacque Vallee, *Messengers of Deception* (Berkeley, California: And/ Or Press, 1974)

11. M. Scott Peck. See "The Road Less Traveled," *Life Times,* Fall-Winter 1986 p. 2; and a *A Different Drum: Community-Making and Peace* (New York: Simon & Schuster, 1988).

12. Jonas Salk. See "Utopia", *Omni* magazine, April 1988; and Barbara Marx-Hubbard, *The Hunger of Eve* (Eastsound, Washington: Island Pacific NW, 1989)

13. I encourage you to acquire and read the following books by Texe Marrs in which Robert Muller is quoted extensively, with complete documentation: *Dark Secrets of the New Age; Mystery Mark of the New Age;* and *Ravaged by the New Age.*

14. Barbara Marx Hubbard, *Happy Birth Day Planet Earth!* (Santa Fe, New Mexico: Ocean Tree Books, 1986); also see Hubbard's book, *The Handbook of Co-Creation.*

15. John Randolph Price, *The Planetary Commission; and Practical Spirituality* (Austin, Texas: Quartus Books, 1985).

16. Matthew Fox. *Original Blessing: A Primer in Creation Spirituality* (Santa Fe, New Mexico: Bear & Company, 1983); and see Fox's heretical 1989 book, *The Coming of the Cosmic Christ* (New York: Harper & Row, Publishers).

17. Reported by Daniel Coleman, "The Mind Over the Body," *The New York Times Magazine,* Sept. 27, 1987.

18. See *The Eagle Forum,* Colorado, May-June 1988, pp. 1, 4. In the foreword to his book, *The Coming of the Cosmic Christ,* New Age Catholic Priest Matthew Fox thanks Laurence Rockefeller for giving him the financial grant that made Fox's book possible.

19. Dotson Rader, "How Marsha Mason Picked Up The Pieces," *Parade* Magazine, June 19, 1988.

20. Michael Crichton, *Travels* (New York: Alfred A. Knopf, 1988).

21. Jeannie Williams, "Cher's Bewildering Soiree For Her Scent," *USA Today,* Nov. 1, 1988, p. 2-D.

22. Norman Vincent Peale, "No More Stress or Tension," *Plus: The Magazine of Positive Thinking,* May, 1986, pp. 22-23. Also see Peale's endorsements on the covers of the New Age, occultic books, *The Jesus Letters,* by Jane Palzere and Anna C. Brown (Newington, Connecticut: 1979); and *The Dead Are Alive: They Can and Do Communicate With You* (New York: Fawcett/Ballantine, 1981).

23. Ibid.

24. Ibid.

25. See *USA Today,* Aug. 23, 1989.

26. "Politics In The New Age," *Fundamentalist Journal,* Oct. 1989, p.65.

27. "Speakers at Choices III," *The Forum,* Aug. 1988, p. 7.

28. Samantha Smith, "Choices III," *The Forum,* Aug. 1988, p. 7.

29. Also see "Royal Medicine," by Dana Ullman, *New Age Journal,* Sept./ Oct. 1987, pp. 45-52, 62.

CHAPTER 3: *The Great Sex Carnival*

1. Advertising flyer for tantric sex retreat, One World Life Services (OWLS), Austin, Texas, 1989.
2. Ibid.
3. *Yoga Journal,* Nov./Dec. 1986, p. 80.
4. See, for example: Arthur Evans, *The God of Ecstasy* (New York: St. Martin's Press, 1988); Linda Fierz-David, *Women's Dionysian Initiation* (Dallas, Texas: Spring Publications, 1988); Miriam Starhawk, *The Spiral Dance: A Rebirth of the Ancient Religian of the Great Goddess* (San Francisco: Harper & Row, Publishers, 1979). Alexander Hislop, *The Two Babylons* (New York: Loizeaux Brothers; 1959 edition); S. Angus, *The Mystery Religions* (New York: Dover Publications, 1928 republished 1975); and Barbara Walker, *The Women's Encyclopedia of Myths and Secrets* (San Francisco: Harper & Row, Publishers, 1983); Robin Lane Fox, *Pagans and Christians* (San Francisco: Harper & Row, Publishers); Sir Wallis Budge, *Egyptian Religion* (New York: Bell Publishing; London ed. 1900); and H. W. F. Saggs, *Everyday Life in Babylonia and Assyria* (New York: Dorset Press, 1965)
5. Alexander Hislop, Ibid.
6. Marilyn Ferguson, *The Aquarian Conspiracy.*
7. Promotional Flyer, "1987 International Seth Seminar," Austin Seth Center, Austin, Texas. Also, see Jane Roberts, *The Seth Material* (Englewood Cliffs, New Jersey: Prentice Hall, 1970) and other "Seth" books.
8. Ibid., p. 83-84
9. Miriam Starhawk, *Yoga Journal,* May-June 1986, p. 59.
10. Miriam Starhawk, *The Spiral Dance: A Rebirth of the Ancient Religion of the Great Goddess* (San Francisco, California: Harper & Row, Publishers, 1979), p. 83.
11. Ibid., p. 83-84.
12. Rita M. Gross, "Hindu Female Deities as a Resource for the Contemporary Rediscovery of the Goddess," *The Book of the Goddess,* edited by Carl Olson (New York: Crossroad Publishing, 1986) pp. 217-229.
13. S. Angus, *The Mystery Religions,* (New York: Dover Publications, 1975 ed.), pp. 112-115.
14. Miriam Starhawk, *The Spiral Dance,* p. 85.
15. Nancy Qualls-Corbett, *The Sacred Prostitute* (Toronto, Canada: Inner City Books, 1988), pp. 58-59, 62-63, 141.
16. Matthew Fox, *Original Blessing* (Santa Fe, New Mexico: Bear & Company, 1983) pp. 282-283.
17. Monica Sjoo and Barara Mor, *The Great Cosmic Mother* (San Francisco, California: Harper & Row 1987)
18. Ibid., p. 54
19. Ibid., p. 221
20. Ibid.
21. Ibid.

22. See *The Book of the Goddess,* edited by Carl Olson, p.18

23. Robert Anton Wilson, *Cosmic Trigger* (Phoenix, Arizona: Falcon Press, 1977), p. 109.

24. Rita Gross in, *The Book of the Goddess,* p. 228.

25. David Wood, *Genesis: The First Book of Revelations* (Tunbridge, Wales; Kent, England: The Baton Press, 1985), p. 107.

26. Irena Tweedle, *The Chasm of Fire,* quoted by Joseph Pearce in *Magical Child Matures* (New York: Bantam Books, 1986).

27. Madonna Kolbenschlag, quoted by Donna Steichen in "The Goddess goes to Washington,"*Fidelity* magazine, December 1986, p. 42.

28. Ibid.

29. Ibid.

30. David Spangler, *The Rebirth of the Sacred* (New York: Delta Books, 1984).

31. Alice Bailey, *A Compilation on Sex* (New York: Lucis Publishing Co., 2nd printing, 1984)

32. Ibid.

33. Alice Bailey, *Ponder on This* (New York: Lucis Trust Publishing Co., 6th printing, 1983).

34. Ibid.

35. Flyer advertising M. Scott Peck Seminar, *Beyond the Road Less Traveled,* Houston, Texas, March 17, 1988.

36. Chris Griscom, *Ecstasy Is A New Frequency* (Santa Fe, New Mexico: Bear & Company, 1987.

37. Ibid

38. Ibid., p. 97

CHAPTER 4: *The Unholy Trinity*

1. Miriam Starhawk, *The Spiral Dance,* p. 29.

2. For an excellent and eye opening discussion of C. S. Lewis' unscriptural views, see the book, *C. S. Lewis on Scripture* (Nashville, Tennessee: Parthenon Press, see especially pp. 75-80), by Michael J. Christensen, an admirer of Lewis!

3. Diane Stein, *The Women's Spirituality Book* (St. Paul, Minnesota: Llewelyn Press, 1987).

4. Robin Westen, *Channelers: A New Age Directory* (New York: Putnam/ Perigee, 1988), p. 95.

5. Bob Fickes, "Planet of Love: The Union of the Heavenly Father and Mother Earth," *Gabriel's Horn* magazine, Summer 1988.

6. David Spangler, *Reflections On The Christ* (Scotland: Findhorn Publications, 1978), pp. 44-45.

7. Bob Fickes, Ibid: pp. 32-33.

CHAPTER 5: Unmasking the Hidden Darkness

1. Kai King, "Bob and Linda," *Gabriel's Horn* magazine, Summer 1988, pp. 34-35.
2. Ibid. 3
3. Ken Carey, *Return of the Bird Tribes* (New York: A Uni*Sun Book, 1988), p. 204.
4. *God Calling*, edited by A. J. Russell, is published in various editions by such publishers as Dodd, Mead & Co., and Barbour and Company.
5. David Wood, *Genesis: The First Book of Revelations*, p. 125.
6. G. H. Pember, *Earth's Earliest Ages* (London: Hodder & Stoughton, 1907).
7. Joseph Campbell, *Accidental Mythology*, as quoted by Richard Roberts in *From Eden to Eros* (San Anselmo, California: Vernal Equinox Press, 1985) p. 29.
8. Vera Alder, *When Humanity Comes of Age* (New York: Samuel Weiser, 1974), pp. 31-32.
9. Kim Miller, "Mother God: Women's Rites and the Tribulation," a special report from *Concerned Christians*, July/August 1987.
10. Paul Twitchell, *The Flute of God* (Crystal, Minnesota: Illuminated Way Publishing, 1969, tenth printing 1988), p. 147.
11. Ibid.
12. Ibid., p. 146
13. William Kingsland, *The Gnosis or Ancient Wisdom in the Christian Scriptures* (London: George Allen and Unwin, Ltd., 1937), p. 93.

CHAPTER 6: Sins of Mystery Babylon

1. See *Halley's Bible Handbook* by Henry B. Halley (Grand Rapids, Michigan: Zondervan, 1965); and the *Bible As History*, by Werner Keller (New York: Bantam Books, 1982).
2. Werner Keller, Ibid., pp. 312-320.
3. Alexander Hislop, *The Two Babylons;* and see the reference in footnote number 4, Chapter 3, for further information about Semiramis, Babylon and the Goddess religion as described in subsequent pages of this chapter.
4. Alexander Hislop, *The Two Babylons*, see pp. 316, 323, 342-358.
5. Ibid, pp. 416-417.
6. Matthew Fox, *Original Blessing* (Santa Fe, New Mexico: Bear & Company, 1983)
7. David Spangler, *Reflections on the Christ* (Scotland: Findhorn Foundation, 1978)
8. Lola Davis, *Toward A World Religion For The New Age* (Farmingdale, New York: Coleman Publishing, 1982).

9. Elizabeth Clark and Herbert Richardson, editors, *Women and Religion: A Feminist Sourcebook of Christian Thought* (New York: Harper & Row, Publishers), pp. 11-12; and see Rosemary Ruether, *Woman Guides* (Boston Beacon Press, 1985), p. 27.
10. Rita M. Gross, *The Book of the Goddess*, pp. 217-230.
11. Mary Daly, *Beyond God the Father*.
12. Merlin Stone, *When God Was A Woman* (New York: Dial Press, 1976)
13. LaVedi Lafferty and Bud Hollowell, *The Eternal Dance* (St. Paul, Minnesota: Llewelyn Publications, 1983).
14. The high tech monthly *Omni* recently stated: "Everyone knows that the left brain hemisphere is rational, logical, and Western, and the right is creative, intuitive and Eastern. Everyone knows, that is, except the scientists..." (See CIB Bulletin, February 1989, p. 1). Also, see the book *Left Brain/Right Brain*, by Sally P. Stringer, in which the author surveys the evidence for separate and independent left and right brain functions and finds "no support" whatever in the scientific community.
15. Ralph Woodrow, *Mystery Babylon Religion*.

CHAPTER 7: *The Goddess Is Back! She Lives!*

1. Paul Twitchell, *The Flute of God*.
2. Monica Sjoo and Barbara Mor, *The Great Cosmic Mother*, pp. 430-431.
3. Ibid.
4. Ibid.
5. Ibid.
6. Leonardo Boff, *The Maternal Face of God* (San Francisco, California: Harper & Row, Publisher, 1987).
7. Ibid., p. 257.
8. Ibid., p. 277.
9. Ibid., preface.
10. Rosemary R. Ruether, *Womanguides: Readings Toward A Feminist Theology* (Boston, Massachusetts: Beacon Press, 1985), p. 213.
11. Ibid., p. 212.
12. Ibid.
13. Ibid., p. 126.
14. Naomi Goldenberg, *Changing of the Gods* (Boston, Massachusetts: Beacon Press, 1979).
15. Ibid.
16. Swami Vivekananda, quoted by Ajit Mookerjee Kali, *The Feminine Force* (New York: Destiny Books, 1988), pp. 79-81.
17. Diane Stein, *The Women's Spirituality Book* (St. Paul, Minnesota: Llewellyn Press, 1987), p.i.
18. Scott Cunningham in Diane Stein book, Ibid.
19. Diane Stein, *The Women's Spirituality Book*, p. 2.
20. Ibid., p. 60.

CHAPTER 8: And Her Son Shall Have The Number 666

1. Robert Muller, *Genesis: Shaping A New Spirituality* (New York: Doubleday/Image Books), p. xiii.
2. Barbara Walker, *The Women's Encyclopedia of Myths and Secrets*, pp. 450-451.
3. Diane Stein, *The Women's Spirituality Book*, p. 26.
4. Miriam Starhawk, *The Spiral Dance*, p. 24.
5. Demetra George, "Mysteries of the Dark Moon," *Woman of Power* magazine, Winter, 1988, pp. 30-31.
6. Maude Reinertsen, *Magical Blend* magazine, Issue #15, 1987, p. 38.
7. Ibid.
8. Quoted by Robert J. Hutchinson, "On the Left," *Catholic Twin Circle*, November 20, 1988, p. 10.
9. Rosemary Ruether quoted by Robert J. Hutchinson, Ibid.
10. Donna Steichen, "The Goddess Goes to Washington, *Fidelity*, December 1986, pp. 34-44.
11. Madonna Kalbenschlag, quoted by Donna Steichen, Ibid.
12. Ibid.
13. Quoted by Donna Steichen, "The Goddess Goes to Washington," *Fidelity*, December 1986, pp. 34-44.
14. Ibid.
15. Matthew Fox, *The Coming of the Cosmic Christ.*
16. Ibid.
17. Foster Bailey, *Running God's Plan*, p. 154.
18. Elwood Babbitt, *Talks With Christ and His Teachers* (Turners Fall, Massachusetts: Fine Line Books, 1981), pp. 114-115.
19. Ibid.
20. See Brian Sibley, *C. S. Lewis: Through the Shadowlands* (Old Tappan, New Jersey: Fleming Revell Company, 1985), pp. 147-148.
21. Regarding C. S. Lewis, see the revealing book by Michael J. Christensen, *C. S. Lewis on Scripture* (Nashville, Abingdon Press, 1979); and C. S. Lewis, *Surprised by Joy* , (San Diego, California: Harcourt Brace Jovanavich, 1956), especially pp. 234-237. Regarding Madeleine L'Engle, see *Eternity* magazine, July/August 1988, p. 38 and *The Wittenberg Door* magazine, 1987, pp. 23-25.
22. Ibid.
23. Madeleine L'Engle, *A Cry Like A Bell* (Harold Shaw Publishers, 1987).
24. Milton Craig, letter published by Colorado's Eagle Forum in *The Forum* newspaper. Also, see "Female Christ Hung in Church," *Christian Inquirer*, June 1984, p. 21.

CHAPTER 9: The Goddess and the Serpent

1. Paul Twitchell, *The Flute of God.*
2. Ibid.

3. Richard Roberts, *From Eden to Eros: Origins of the Put Down of Women* (San Anselmo, California: Vernal Equinox Press, 1985), p.6.
4. Ibid., p. 24
5. Ibid., p. 10
6. Ibid
7. Mary Daley, *Beyond God The Father* (Boston, 1973), p. 96.
8. Ibid.
9. Ken Carey, *Return of the Bird Tribes*
10. Ibid., p. 171
11. F. Aster Barnwell, *The Meaning of Christ for Our Age* (St. Paul, Minnesota: Llewellyn Publications, 1984).
12. As quoted by James Sire in *Twisting Scripture* (Downers Grove, Illinois: Inter Varsity Press, 1980) p. 160.
13. Elizabeth Clare Prophet, *The Great White Brotherhood in the Culture History, & Religion of America* (Livingston, Montana: Summit University Press).
14. Ibid.
15. John Randolph Price, from the "World Day of Healing Prayer," The *Planetary Commission* (Austin, Texas: Quartus Books, 1984)
16. Ralph Woodrow, *Babylon Mystery Religion* (Riverside, California: Ralph Woodrow Evangelistic Association, 1981 ed.)
17. *The Book of the Goddess,* ed. by Carl Olson
18. Alexandra Kovats, "Reclaiming Serpent Power," *Creation,* Sept./Oct. 1988.

CHAPTER 10: *The One Most Terrible Secret*

1. Rosemary Ruether, *Womanguides,* pp. 212-213.
2. Bob Fickes, "Planet of Love. . ." *Gabriel's Horn,* Summer 1988.
3. Ken Carey, *The Return of the Bird Tribes,* pp. 55-242; also see pp. 195-233.
4. Ibid., p. 231.
5. Ibid., p. 233.
6. Ibid.,
7. Z. Budapest, "Political Witchcraft," *Woman of Power* magazine, Winter 1988, p. 38.
8. Naomi Goldenberg, quoted by Pauline G. MacPherson, *Can The Elect Be Deceived?* (Colorado: Bold Truth Press, 1986), p. 178.
9. Ibid.
10. Matthew Fox, *The Coming of the Cosmic* Christ, p. 61.
11. Ken Carey, *The Return of the Bird Tribes,* p. 57; and see pp. 152, 184, 196.
12. Ibid.
13. Ibid., p 146
14. Ibid., pp. 145-146
15. Ibid., pp. 152-153
16. Leonardo Boff, *The Maternal Face of God,* pp. 234-235
17. Carl Jung, quoted by Leonardo Boff, Ibid.

18. Julie Bowden and Herbert Gravitz, *Guide To Recovery: A Book For Adult Children of Alcoholics* (Holmes Beach, Florida: Learning Publications, 1985).
19. Geoffrey Parrinder, *Sex and World Religions* (London: Sheldon Press, 1980), pp. 36-37.
20. Miriam Starhawk, *The Spiral Dance.*
21. Ken Carey, *Return of the Bird Tribes,* p. 57.

CHAPTER 11: Initiation: The Seduction of Women

1. Miriam Starhawk, *The Spiral Dance,* p. 149.
2. Ibid., p. 85.
3. Ibid.
4. Ibid., pp. 28, 195.
5. Ibid., p. 14.
6. Ibid., p. 188
7. Christopher J. Maier, "Peace Pilgrim," *Meditation* magazine, Fall 1989, p. 16.
8. Ken Carey, *Return of the Bird Tribes,* p. 195.
9. Ibid., pp. 195-200
10. Ibid., p. 196.
11. Ibid., pp. 197-198.
12. Ibid., p. 200.
13. Ibid., p. 55.
14. Ibid., p. 226.

CHAPTER 12: You, Too, Can Become A Goddess

1. Alice Bailey, *Ponder On This,* pp. 15, 278-279.
2. Miriam Starhawk, *The Spiral Dance,* pp. 76-77.
3. Ibid., p. 77.
4. Alice Bailey, *Esoteric Psychology* I (New York: Lucis Trust, 9th Printing, 1979), pp. 284-285.
5. Ibid., p. 285.
6. Ibid.
7. Whitley Strieber, *Communion* (New York: William Morrow, 1987)
8. Richard Roberts, *From Eden to Eros,* p. 65.
9. Ibid.

CHAPTER 13: The Lifestyle of the Liberated Aquarian Woman

1. Christina Thomas, *Secrets: A Practical Guide to Undreamed of Possibilities* (Memphis, Tennessee: Chela Publications, 1989), p. 131.

2. Ibid., pp. 161-162.
3. Ibid.
4. Ibid., pp. 123-124.
5. Ibid.
6. Ibid.
7. See Merlin Stone, *When God Was A Woman,* pp. 42-44; Walter Burkert, *Greek Religion* (Cambridge, Massachusetts: Harvard University Press); Gerald A. Larue, Long Beach, California: Centerline Press, 1988); and Robin Lane Fox, *Pagans and Christians* (San Francisco, California: Harper & Row, Publishers, 1986).
8. Ibid.
9. Merlin Stone, *When God Was A Woman,* pp. 42-44.
10. Melody Beattie, *Co-dependent No More* (New York: Harper & Row, Publishers, 1987), pp. 114-115.
11. Ibid.
12. Ibid., p. 156.
13. Walter Burkert, *Greek Religions,* p. 292.
14. Margot Adler, *Drawing Down the Moon* (Boston: Beacon Press, 1986).

CHAPTER 14: Back to the Future

1. Chris Griscom, *Ecstasy is a New Frequency,* pp. 95-96.
2. Ibid., pp. 123-125.
3. John Randolph Price, *Practical Spirituality* (Austin, Texas: Quartus Books, 1985), p. 20.
4. Linda Clark, *et al, Image Breaking, Image Building* (New York, 1984), pp. 47-48.
5. See William Oddie, *What Will Happen To God?* (San Francisco, California: Ignatius Press, 1988), pp. 3-5.
6. Toni Kosydar, "The Seth Material," promotional flyer advertising Seth workshops and seminars. This same flyer discussed Jane Roberts' speaking in tongues.
7. Jane Gross, "With Guru Departed, Disciples Struggle On," *New York Times,* January 25, 1989.
8. Ibid.
9. Murray Hope, *Practical Celtic Magic* (England: The Aquarian Press, 1987), pp. 146-158. For additional evidence regarding the pagan, occultic roots of Taliesin, Arthur, and Merlin, see: Alan Richardson and Geoff Hughes, *Ancient Magick for a New Age: Rituals From the Merlin Temple and the Magick of the Dragon Kings* (St. Paul, Minnesota: Llewellyn Press, 1989); Nikolai Tolstoy, *The Quest for Merlin* (Boston: Little, Brown & Co., 1985); Gareth Knight, *The Secret Tradition in Arthurian Legend* (England: The Aquarian Press, 1983); *Gnosis* magazine, Summer 1989, pp. 76-78, and *Magical Blend* magazine, through January 1990, pp. 76-79.
10. Ibid.
11. Manley P. Hall, *The Secret Teachings of All Ages* (Los Angeles: Philosophical Research Society), pp. XXII-XXIII.

12. Steven Lawhead, *Taliesin* (Westchester, Illinois: Crossway Books, 1987).
13. John Sharkey, *Celtic Mysteries: The Ancient Religion* (New York: Thames and Hudson, 1979), p. 6.
14. Alexander Hislop, *The Two Babylons,* p. 103.
15. John Sharkey, *Celtic Mysteries: The Ancient Religion,* p.8.
16. Ibid.
17. Ibid., p. 10.
18. Ibid., p. 15.
19. Page Bryant, *Wildfire* magazine, Vol. 4, No. 3, 1989, p. 37.
20. Ibid.
21. Ibid.

About the Author

Wanda Marrs is co-founder of Living Truth Ministries, and the Association to Rescue Kids (ARK).

She has appeared on radio and television stations across America, exposing the New Age movement and explaining God's wonderful plan for Christian women.

Prior to entering full-time ministry work with her husband, bestselling author Texe Marrs, Wanda had a long and varied career, starting off as a professional secretary and being promoted into higher management. She served as Director of Development and Community Relations for one of the largest hospitals in Arizona, Tucson General Hospital, and also co-founded Tech Trends, a high-tech consulting firm.

In addition to authoring *New Age Lies to Women*, Wanda has co-authored four other books, including *Secretary Today, Manager Tomorrow*, and *High Tech Job-Finder*.

Wanda is mother of two grown children and is grandmother of three including a precious set of twins. She lives in Austin, Texas with her husband.

For Our Newsletter

Texe and Wanda Marrs offer a free newsletter about Bible prophecy, the New Age movement, cults, the occult challenge to Christianity, rescuing our children and other important topics.

If you would like to receive this newsletter, please write to:

Living Truth Ministries
8103-N Shiloh Court
Austin, TX 78745

From Texe Marrs -- Now Available at Your Bookstore

Books

RAVAGED BY THE NEW AGE: Satan's Plan to Destroy Our Kids

MYSTERY MARK OF THE NEW AGE: Satan's Design for World Domination

DARK SECRETS OF THE NEW AGE: Satan's Plan for a One World Religion

MEGA FORCES: Signs and Wonders of the Coming Chaos

Videos

TEXE MARRS EXPOSES SATAN'S NEW AGE PLAN FOR A ONE WORLD ORDER: Is the Reign of Antichrist Just Ahead?

Tapes

NIGHT COMETH!
The New Age Beast and His Riders of Death

NIGHTSOUNDS:
The Hidden Dangers of New Age Music